Seduction

The Ultimate Guide on How to Attract, flirt with, and Seduce Women Using your Attractive Alpha Male Personality, Including Dating Tips to Get a Girlfriend who will Pine for You

Contents

Introduction

Seduction may seem an old-fashioned term when applied to modern dating, but it is what most women are looking for. Dating has become a minefield for men, and it can be hard to know what is acceptable now. This book has all the answers you need to get women interested, keep them interested, and make them chase you instead of the other way around.

Nature demonstrates that alpha males' rule. They have the pick of the females, the best food, and are the protectors of their tribe. Why would it be any different for men? Women have an inbuilt need for an alpha male. They may not even know it, but they are hardwired to seek out male perfection to mate with.

Discover how to become that specimen. Learn the tricks that will ensure you have women falling at your feet. Use your charm and personality to win over the most attractive women and have them hanging on your every word. There are strategies and tips for every situation.

This book is packed with strategies that can be used by every man, depending on their strengths. Some of the information may seem conflicting, but what works for you may not work for the next man. Alpha males do not all come in one-size-fits-all packages. They can be the typical bad boy who women find fascinating, but are ultimately not partner material. Or they can be the guy who looks like a rock and is also the best listener a girl has ever met.

Have you ever considered online dating? What are the best sites to use? How do you create a profile to attract the most attention? Even if you have never considered this form of dating, you will soon be able to make the leap online. In a matter of hours, you can be swiping right like an expert!

Being an alpha male does not mean that you cannot be a good guy. Chivalry and good manners can be a huge turn-on for some women. One of the key things you will learn is how to identify what type of women are out there and what they are looking for. Knowledge is power, and this applies to the dating scene as well as life. Develop a radar for women that will help you find the woman of your dreams.

Flirting is an art. Combine fearless flirting with sexually charged body language, and you are a walking come-on to beautiful chicks. They will welcome your attention and return your flirting. Banter and appropriate physical contact will soon lead to the bedroom. Making people feel better about themselves is also an art that will help you find success in life. Flirting is another way to make women feel special, and you can use your art to seduce them.

Natural leadership will become second nature to you. Improve your work life, social life, and love life. Always have a sense of purpose and know what to expect from life. You will never knowingly accept second best once you have mastered the techniques in this book. Why should you? Second best is for omega and beta males, and you have risen through those ranks.

Finally, you will understand what it takes to be the man all men want to be; the man all women want to bed and the man they will do anything to get. The iron rules of man will help you remember what is important and what should be avoided.

So, are you ready to start your new life? Jump on in and begin your journey to successful dating. The world of women is out there just waiting for your fine self to arrive!

Part One: Women and What They Want

Battle of the Sexes

It is an anthropological fact that men and women are different, and brain scans, controlled studies, and evolutionary psychology further attest to this. These differences are both mental and physical. The two sexes absorb information, process it, and then act on it in separate ways. Male and female hormones also mean that men and women have different priorities, which often results in a misaligned view of the world. This can create conflict in several aspects of their lives.

If you can understand these differences, then you can interact with more empathy. Physical elements govern gender behavior, but it is also subject to learned and enacted experiences.

The Differences Between Male and Female Brains

Larry Cahill, Ph.D., has studied the human brain for decades and has some mind-blowing conclusions. Back in 2000, he scanned the brains of both men and women when watching films that were either highly aversive or negatively emotional. The results indicated that women retain emotional experiences to a higher degree than men. This can trigger richer, more intense memories, and leave them susceptible to anxiety and depression.

The male brain activity was also more tightly coordinated and restricted to just one side of the brain. The female brain, when shown an emotional image, lit up nine different areas of the brain, while the male brain only lit up two. Male brains further use more testosterone and vasopressin, while female brains use estrogen and oxytocin.

Male and Female Emotions

Women recognize sadness in a facial expression 90 percent of the time, while men do so only 40 percent of the time. Dr. Louann Brizendine MD wrote in her book *The Female Brain* that women are four times more likely to cry when confronted with sadness. This is because the female brain recognizes that men need a visual display of sadness to provoke empathy.

Regarding evolution, it makes more sense for women to have highly developed facial expression reading skills as they need to recognize the non-verbal cues of babies.

Male and Females are not Empathetic in the Same Way

The human body has two emotional systems. The first is the mirror neuron system (MNS), which is responsible for how empathy controls the way people react to others and share their feelings. It controls our empathy and sympathetic emotions. The second system is the temporal-parietal junction (TPJ), which instructs the brain to distance itself from emotional focus and instead search for a practical way to address the situation.

Studies have shown that both male and female brains begin the empathy process in MNS, but the male brain will swiftly cross over to TPJ as it feels that time spent discussing it and sharing feelings will be wasted time. The male answer to the problem will be along the lines of more practical solutions.

The Institute of Neurology in London conducted some research into emotional empathy in the sexes and produced the following results. They carried out tests on couples, taking the women first and subjecting them to a series of electric shocks. They then took the men, connected them to the same machines, and removed the females from the testing area. It was indicated to the women that their respective partners were undergoing the same types of shocks. Even though the females could not see or hear their partners, the areas of their brain that had activated during their period of being shocked, lit up when their partner underwent the same treatment. The brain indicated that they suffered the same level of pain by just imagining their partner's discomfort – the same pain they endured when being shocked. Unsurprisingly, when the roles were reversed, the results showed little or no empathy.

Males are Aroused by Stress

Men get a real kick out of stressful or aggressive situations. Whereas females will react entirely differently. Looking at these facts from an evolutionary perspective, this makes sense. If a woman's brain is faced with a stressful, unstable situation, it is highly unlikely that she will want to have sex, which may lead to pregnancy. A woman will only feel comfortable enough to procreate in a calm and balanced environment. The male brain, however, is telling him to procreate with multiple partners and increase the chance of preserving his genetic line in times of danger.

Orgasms Affect Male and Females Differently

When a female orgasms, the hormones oxytocin and dopamine are released. She then feels content and secure and wants to share that feeling with her man by cuddling or spooning. When a man ejaculates, his brain is flooded with neurochemicals that incite intense emotional responses. He then enters a phase of resolution and refraction, which will lead to drowsiness. These chemicals directly affect his sleep center and trigger intense feelings of tiredness.

Interesting fact: The arched back syndrome of orgasm is purely a female thing!

Men Tend to Fall in Love at First Sight

Contrary to popular belief, it is men who fall quicker and harder! Women's brains are set up to err on the side of caution. They know that they need to assess a male's ability to protect them and provide for their futures. Men, on the other hand, will see what they want and decide, there and then, they want to have children with a woman based purely on her physical attributes.

Interesting fact: Therefore, guys who are looking to "pick up" surround themselves with pretty women. They are using a strategy called preselection. This means they are giving the impression they have been vetted and approved by the bevy of beauties that surround them.

Men are Attracted to Youth and Beauty While Women are Attracted to Status

Psychologist David Buss studied over 10,000 different individuals from over 35 different cultures. He found that no matter who you are and where you are, some things are universal when it comes to attraction. These preferences have governed the way people choose a mate ever since the human species evolved.

Men are attracted by:
- Symmetry
- Youth
- Radiant signs of healthiness and fertility

Women are attracted by:
- Symmetry
- Success in the workplace
- Older men
- Taller men
- Generous nature
- Kindness
- Interest in children
- Trustworthiness

Interesting fact: These factors will still apply to females who are completely financially secure. They will still seek out secure men.

Men Do the Chasing; Women are Chased

Some people will argue this point, but it is a universal fact that females are coy, and males are blessed with sexual boldness. Take, for example, tribal cultures that are completely untouched by Western cultures. Men pursue women, and there is a simple reasoning behind this phenomenon. Sperm is readily available, and eggs are a limited resource. Women only have several attempts to produce offspring due to the time restraints and physical toll it takes on their bodies.

Men, however, are unlimited as to how many women they can sleep with.

Men's Sex Drive is Affected by the People Who Surround Them

American journalist Robert Wright wrote in his novel *The Moral Animal* that men's sperm count increases significantly when they are away from their partner. If he has multiple sexual partners, it will replenish following each copulation. If he remains faithful to his partner and restricts his sexual activity to her, his sperm count will be depleted following each coupling. This is because his body is hardwired to produce offspring with as many women as possible. A woman's body, however, will remain constant no matter how many partners she has. Her egg count is determined at birth, and her ovulation cycles are in no way affected by her environment. Put simply, even if One Direction and Henry Cavill are waiting on her hand and foot, she will not be affected from a fertility point of view.

Men and Women's Brains Age Differently

Men lose more of their cortex at a faster speed than women – essentially, they lose their gray matter quicker than women. This is why certain disorders like Parkinson's are more likely to affect men.

Men and Women View Cleaning Differently

The kitchen is the heart of the house, and women know that if the kitchen is messy, the whole house is affected. They know that if they do not do it, then no one will. Men, conversely, seem to think pixies come in the night and clear up messes. They believe that a messy room shows they are comfortable with their eco-warrior side. Women, however, are less likely to be bothered by a dirty car. It is not in the house, so why would she be bothered? Men, however, think a shiny car is a status symbol. They can spend hours waxing and polishing their vehicle even though they consider ten minutes doing the washing up beneath them!

These are not hard rules, but they are important insights into male and female psyches. They do show that one's sex is accompanied by a blueprint, which affects how one behaves.

What Women Really Want from Men

When you are looking for a relationship, you need to know what the other person is seeking. It does not matter if you are looking for a quick hookup, a casual relationship, or your soulmate. In essence, you need to know what women are looking for.

Women are ultimately relationship orientated and looking for the following qualities in men:

1) Emotional stability. Women need a rock in their life. They need a man who will be there for them, have their back, and give them a feeling of safety when they are vulnerable. Men who have drastic mood swings may be interesting as friends or even on-screen, but not many women will want them as a mate. If you blow hot and cold, she won't know where she is. Maintain a rock-like persona and show her you can be depended on.

2) Honesty, but not brutal. Women who are committed to their men believe they exist as one. Therefore, they expect you to be honest about important stuff. They also expect you to admit when you are wrong and can show when you are hurt. Men who become defensive and storm off are emotionally unstable. Talking things through is an important part of a successful relationship. If you can show a woman you are willing to share good and bad experiences in your life, they will be more willing to let you in. However, they are not open to brutal honesty! When they ask if they look good in an outfit or if you like their new haircut, the answer is always yes! In fact, this is the only sort of stuff you can lie about. Don't tell her that she looks like crap (even if she does!).

3) **Understanding.** Women want their men to know them completely. The air of mystery is a veil that lures men in but is quickly cast to one side. A woman is keen to form bonds that mean you know her inside out – ask her how she feels, and why she is affected by certain situations. The real person inside of her, not the persona she shows to the world, will want validation. Everyone needs reminding why they are lovable, and the way to do this is to understand a woman on every level. Don't lie about your real personality, as the hurt you will cause will be irreparable. Be true to her, and she will reward you with unbreakable loyalty.

4) **Care for her.** Showing you care can be seen as a weakness by some, but in reality, it is one of the strongest emotions available. When you listen and respect her beliefs, you show a high level of care. For instance, she decides she is going on a vegan and gluten-free diet, yet you are due to eat out the following evening. If you ring the restaurant ahead of time and make sure she has a choice of dishes to choose from, you are showing you care. This avoids any embarrassment on her part if she finds she can't eat there.

5) **Respect.** Never make fun of women. Even if you disagree with their opinions, you should respect them. Never poke fun at their weight, hair, or aging process, especially in public. You may have playful banter you use at home, but that should never be aired in public. Derogatory remarks won't just make her feel uncomfortable; they will make you look like an ass!

6) **Be affectionate.** Nobody is suggesting you hump her leg like some sort of sex-crazed dog, but a simple touch on the neck will make her feel special. Just linking her finger with yours will show her you need to feel connected if only momentarily. Even when you are

separated across a crowded room, make sure you make eye contact with her and form a silent bond.

7) Be fun. Women love men who are willing to let down their barriers and show their fun side. The best couples will often tell you they are each other's best friend. They love to spend time together and share jokes, a zest for life, and common interests. If she is interested in funny cat videos and finds them hilarious, try and see what she means. You may find that a common love for Grumpy cat will help you bond! Who knows? Maybe you could try a date with a difference. Forget about going to a bar or restaurant for the evening and check out any local amusement park or carnivals. They will show you have imagination, a sense of fun, and that you want to share every experience with her.

8) Confidence combined with humility. Confidence is possibly the sexiest quality a man can possess. When you know your self-worth, it shows. The way you walk, talk, and interact with people shows her you are a catch. When you combine this with a sense of humility, you are on the way to becoming the complete package. It's all about loving yourself and knowing when to walk away from toxicity and the things in life that drain your spirit.

9) Open to ideas. Men who think they know it all are not attractive to women. They are looking for men who are curious, always reading, or learning new things. If you show interest in new stuff, you are showing your willingness to come out of your comfort zone, and that is attractive!

10) Blind loyalty. Everyone has an ego; some are bigger than others, of course. Men and women both expect their partners to see them as the best partner they could ever wish for. Women know their restrictions. A woman may accept that she is not the most beautiful, smart, or sexy woman in the world, but she doesn't need to be. She just needs you to believe that she is the best in the world for you. Tell her that she is special, and she will love you for it.

Hot Chick vs. Cold Chick

Hot chicks make the world a better place, right? But what exactly constitutes a hot chick? And why, when there are so many hot chicks out there, do men choose to pursue the cold chicks? What is it about these ice queens that make men's legs go wobbly and their tongues loll out like a thirsty dog? You will explore that conundrum later, but for now, learn more about this favorite subject!

Women come in many forms; curvy, sexy, pretty, urban, foxy, refined, streetwise, and sultry, along with a thousand other adjectives. Men look at women as an object first and a person second. What can you actually do when you spot a hot chick across a room? Take the time to check out her fine ass or peer into her soul? The former might sound crass, but it's reasonable.

The media has a big influence on how men see the perfect woman. At the moment, bronzed bodies with huge chests, hair extensions, and an ass that can knock over a child are the favored look for women. Sexuality is being marketed as a package that is all about false eyelashes and pouty lips.

However, as a man, what do you find hot? Do you like the natural look? A woman who works out can appeal to your need to procreate and create amazing children. Look at the types of women who rise above the standard male fantasy and why that alone classes them as hot. Women are stunning creatures with assets that can be both unique and enchanting.

Take a different look at what makes women hot:

● **How she speaks.** This can be interpreted in two different ways. If you find a smart woman who speaks her mind, you will also know that smart women have passion. They care about the things that excite them, and if one of the things is you, then you are in for a passionate ride! You can also tell the hotness of a woman by the vocabulary she uses. Some women can make a shopping list seem like the Kama Sutra! Do they sound breathy when they are talking to you? That's hot, right? Do they use double meanings in a subtly sexy way? Again hot! The mouth can play a huge part in determining a woman's hotness, and that's before you hit the bedroom!

● **Age.** Some men dismiss women of a certain age and instead pursue young women. What they are doing is dismissing all those years of experience and expertise in favor of a tight body. What is hot about an older woman is the way her body and mind have survived everything that has been thrown at her for so many years. She will teach you stuff that never appears in sex guides! She will have patience and tricks to make even the most nervous man a stud within minutes. Older women appreciate a man who recognizes their appeal. So next time you meet a lady who might be able to give you a few tips, don't dismiss her as a cougar. Hot doesn't diminish with age. Have you seen Cindy Crawford or Demi Moore lately?

● **The one-night stand type of girl.** It is surely every man's dream to have anonymous sex at least once in their life. Do you dream of spotting someone in a room or bar, exchanging looks, and then a couple of words before ripping each other's clothes off and spending the night having hot sex? If a woman is dressed to impress and makes the first move, then you may be in luck. Watch for a moderately sized group of women and then spot the ones who are actively flirting. Is the woman you have spotted looking hot and available? Is she giving you the eye? Talk to her – she may be looking for the same experience you are, and there is really only one way to find out!

13

- **Ambition.** If you find a woman who will stop at nothing to achieve her dreams, then that is one hot lady. She isn't going to let others get in her way, and passion and determination are her go-to emotions. If you can attract such a woman, then your life will be filled with red-hot passion and commitment.

- **She is a fierce best friend.** Women who love to build people up instead of bringing them down are hot! They have the self-confidence to celebrate other successes without feeling envy or bitterness. She is an optimist who views the world with hope, and she will make your world a better place.

- **Women who aren't needy.** Do you want to spend time with your friends doing guy stuff? Do you need to have alone time to cope with stress at work? So, if you find a woman who recognizes these needs, then that is a hot quality. You will probably also like to find a woman who doesn't appear overly dependent on you. When couples have separate interests, it means they have more to talk about when they get together.

- **She loves sex.** The Hottest trait of all! For decades, women were told that enjoying themselves in the bedroom was taboo. They were taught that sex was all about babies, and any woman that enjoyed that sort of thing was, essentially, a tramp. Luckily, those attitudes are strictly in the past. Women who enjoy sex now share that information in a healthy, shame-free manner, and that is hot. Find yourself a sexually liberated woman and climb aboard for the ride (pun intended)!

Why do some chicks act cold?

You know the scene well; you enter a room and then spot her. The amazing looking woman with the hottest body you have ever seen. She is dressed to kill and has an air about her that screams, "Look at me." So, you catch her eye, give her your sexy smile, and then.... nothing. She snubs you and turns back to her friends with a look of disdain.

Why does that happen? Well, there many theories about beautiful women and why they act like that. Usually, they are bored with men hitting on them, tired of being approached based on their looks, or maybe they have just had a bad day. However, that type of behavior, although understandable, is not acceptable to most men. You are not a creep who is trying to pick her up; you just want to make a connection.

So, what do you do next?

Approach her and give her a chance to lower her shield. A simple "Hi, how are you?" will give you an indication of her attitude. If she responds with a friendly reply, then go for it, carry on the conversation. However, if she gives you an attitude, then you need to respond accordingly.

Being rude is not acceptable, and you need to call her out on her behavior. You need to tell her that she may be pretty, but you are a human being who deserves respect.

Try the following responses:

- Smile, tilt your head quizzically, and say, "Goodbye."
- Smile, respond with the phrase, "Wow, I don't know where you were raised, but my parents brought me up to have better manners than that," and then turn and leave.
- Smile, say, "Thanks for saving me time and effort. You are clearly not worth the effort," and leave.
- Smile, laugh, and do your best surprised face, then leave.

You are not looking for crumbs from anyone's table. You know you are a good guy, and you deserve better than that. If she cannot be nice, then you haven't got the time to bother with her. There are plenty of women out there who are worthy of your interest, and she just took herself out of the game.

What happens next?

Well, experience suggests that there is a good chance she will be so shocked by your response she will come after you.

"What, are you serious?" you might ask.

After all, Darwin nailed it when he described women's reactions to certain situations. You just broke through her barrier and refused to be cowed by her ice queen persona. Now the tables have turned.

She now realizes that she wants to know more about you. She did not expect that reaction, and she is now intrigued by your standards, your reality, and honesty. She is used to men just wilting before her, and now she wants what she cannot have.

Your reaction has shown her that her actions have consequences. But it is not about teaching her a lesson; it's about your standards and intolerance to rude behavior. She may ask you why you are leaving or if you want to stay. Tell her politely that she is not a friendly girl, and you are not interested in playing games. Simple, right?

The trick is you need to mean it. You are a good guy who deserves a friendly girl. There are plenty of nice, friendly girls out there just waiting for a decent man to connect with. That is how you approach cold chicks. Be a man and assert your values. That is true alpha male behavior. There is no need to act overtly macho or be rude to women; you are just true to yourself.

Dating Women in the Digital Age

This is a contentious subject because it covers such a vast array of information. You may be looking for a long-term relationship, a dominatrix to administer punishment or just someone to go to the cinema with. The dizzying selection of apps, dating sites, websites, and solo predators makes it difficult to choose how to connect and disconnect with other people, i.e., women!

Check Out Facebook and Twitter

Most people will enter the social media dating experience expecting to meet a stranger. The truth is that you are more likely to connect with someone who is just one or two degrees away from you. Friends of friends, people who hang out with workmates, or friends of the family can all provide you with a potential dating pool.

First, you must realize that if you message a woman who is friends with someone, you know their first reaction will be to ask them about you. So, choose female friends who actually like you and scroll through their friends' lists. If you see someone who looks attractive, the next thing to do is to message her.

You can go the long way around and begin by liking her posts and then commenting on them, but that can take time. Sending her a message right off the bat shows you are keen to know her better. Start with a "Hey, how are you?" or a simple wave. You can use an open lie that hurts no one. This can be a better ice breaker and start a conversation. Try "Hey, did I meet you last weekend at the bar in town? Where you with (insert friends name)?" and wait for her reply.

This type of approach is quite obviously BS, and she will react in one of three ways. She will ignore you, and there will be no reaction at all. She will play along and reply positively and maybe suggest you want to meet up again at the same bar. Or, she will call you on it, and you can hold your hands up and say you just thought she looked cute.

From there, the rest is up to you both. You can carry on messaging and responding to posts without ever meeting, or you can take the bull by the horns and go on a date. Once you start messaging, you will get a better idea about how much you want to get to know her better.

Whatever you do, social media provides a platform for 'testing the waters' without facing social embarrassment or public humiliation. You can limit yourself to a few messages before suggesting you speak on the phone. Text can be limiting when it comes to judging someone's personality, but just hearing a woman's laugh on the phone will tell you if you could possibly get on.

Facebook and Twitter will give you plenty of opportunities to form connections with attractive women. You can see pictures and posts that will provide you with plenty of information about them. This type of social media is also more likely to be a real interpretation of the person posting. They are interacting with friends and family, so they will keep it real or run the risk of being called out as fake.

The same cannot be said of dating apps and websites. This is a whole new ballgame where you will need to have your wits about you and know all the best tips and tricks.

How to Choose a Dating App

Dating used to be tough – going to a bar or an event, meeting women who may or may not be interested in you, hoping your friends or family will know someone who they think is your type and arranging to meet them. Blind dates, personal ads, and bar hopping are mostly a thing of the past, too.

Online dating used to have negative feedback and was believed to be awash with creeps and perverts looking for like-minded partners. Nowadays, the technology available means that online dating is now the norm. You have a huge choice of sites to choose from, some that work for you and some that do not. You need to select the ones that suit you and your expectations.

Here are some popular sites and how they work:

Match

This online dating service has websites that cover over 50 countries, a dozen languages, and has around 30 million members. It is a powerful search tool that matches you with women whose profiles are compatible with yours. Their mission is to keep you safe with a vigorous profile verification process. They also have extensive personal data protection and are committed to giving you the best online dating experience available.

You have full control over your contacts and can use the three options to filter who you can connect with. You can use the "Blacklist" function to block members or use the "Unavailable" mode to browse the site without being detected. The contact filter allows you to select criteria that must be met before a member can contact you.

The site has perfected its algorithm over the last 20+ years, and it's considered one of the best performing websites for dating. You can begin with a 100 percent free membership, where you can create a profile, browse without limits, and use the different flirting tools available. These include Likes and Winks with limited messaging. If you like what you see, you can upgrade your account to get full access.

Their subsidiaries include PlentyofFish, Tinder, OkCupid, and SpeedDate.com, including others.

eHarmony

Launched in 2000, this is a website that is designed for those with the desire for a long-term relationship or marriage. If you are looking for a hookup or something more casual, then eHarmony is not for you. It is also a recommended site for practicing Christians as a significant number of its members identify as Christians.

Initially, you take the 29 Dimensions of Compatibility questionnaire and then let the website do the rest. They will message you every time the site finds someone who they think will share your passions. Once again, it is free to try, and if you like what you see, you can subscribe.

Zoosk

This is a fun site that originated on Facebook in 2007 but is now a worldwide dating phenomenon. It attracts the younger spectrum of singletons and gives members a range of tools to integrate networking and dating. It has members in over 80 countries and is available in 25 languages. It boasts over 40 million members and embraces diversity.

Their system uses a carousel show to display pictures that may appeal to you and asks users to vote yes or no or maybe. They match people according to age, location, height, religion, body type, and other criteria. You can send a smile or like for free, but messaging requires a subscription.

OurTime

Aimed at mature men looking to meet women who are the same age as them, OurTime has appealing features for men of all ages. If you are a younger man looking to connect with a more mature lady, then this could be the site for you. Alternatively, if you are a mature man looking for age-specific ladies, then jump right in.

The site appreciates that the older generation is not as tech-savvy as younger people and guides users through its processes. You can create a profile right away but are given the option to come back later and update it. It recognizes that more mature users will need to become comfortable with the process before imparting personal details.

There are well written, simple to understand articles on the site explaining online dating and the pitfalls it can throw up. The support team is always available to help and is just an email or phone call away. Safety is also paramount at OurTime, and it has a ton of tools to protect your online details. You will remain anonymous until you decide to introduce yourself to someone else.

BlackPeopleMeet

Gender and race are the top two dating identifiers, so it makes perfect sense to create a site for single black men and women to meet. Created in 2002, it is a sister site to Match.com, so you know you are in good hands! Their vast dating network includes a variety of interracial, ethnic, and diverse members who recognize the need for a site filled with great profiles attached to real people.

They have a great pre-scripted option for messages that give the nervous user an option to use. Starting a conversation with new people can be daunting, and these pre-scripted options are ideal. You can use the Matchme option to place yourself in other people's Daily Matches to see if the interest is reciprocated.

Signing up for BlackPeopleMeet is simple. Age, email, and a username, and you are in. As time passes and you become more confident on the site, you can add details. The site also provides example answers to give you an idea about what to put in your profile. Aside from the normal subscription charges, you can also buy tokens to send virtual gifts to any members who you feel connected with.

Of course, these are just a few of the sites out there, but you get the idea. The one thing they all have in common is the need to create a profile that includes at least one picture.

How to Create the Perfect Online Dating Profile

1) **Choose the best pictures**: Action shots are among the most appealing photos when women are considering online dates. Even if they don't show your face, they demonstrate your talents – downhill skiing, cycling, playing the guitar, whatever it is, it will attract more likes and messages than a standard picture. You should also include a picture of you smiling. Most men will choose a sexy pout for their profile picture, but they can look ridiculous. Women will respond to a happy, open smile that makes you look accessible. Always choose recent pictures! Yes, you probably looked better ten

years ago, but you will eventually meet the women who are viewing your picture, and they will appreciate the honesty of a recent snap.

2) Ask your friends for help: They know you the best. They may even point out some positive aspects of your personality that you are unaware of! Often your friends know you better than you know yourself.

3) Be positive: Your profile is not the place to reveal any negative points about yourself. This is essentially your dating C.V. and should be packed with positivity. List things that excite you, along with your positive personality traits. If you love cooking, then name the recipes you consider your signature dishes. Being specific about stuff will bring you to life for anyone reading.

4) Have fun: Show your natural sense of humor in your profile. Include a humorous angle to your profile and show your sense of fun. You may have a quirky hobby that highlights your fun side. Use humor, and the ladies will soon be checking out your DM box!

5) Tell people what you want: Honesty should be the theme of your profile, especially when stating your expectations. If you are looking for a friend to share evenings with on a casual basis, then say so. If you are in a place where you are ready to settle down and have kids, then say so.

6) Be original: Try and steer away from old clichéd lines. Cuddling while watching Netflix is so last year! When you are compiling your profile, take a look at other people's and get some tips from them. Google the best profiles on Tinder and learn from them! There are some excellent profiles out there, and you can pick up some awesome tips!

The key to a killer profile is to outline your best bits. If you have a ripped body, then include at least one photo that shows it off. You are competing with a lot of other men, and you need to stand out.

Humor, intelligence, great pictures, and honesty will soon have the ladies swiping right!

Part Two: Alpha Male Strategies

What Makes a Man Attractive and What Doesn't?

There is someone for everyone, right? Every hole has a corresponding peg. But what makes that peg right for her hole? If you want to stand out in a crowd, then you need to know what makes you attractive to women and what does not.

Qualities That Women Find Attractive

- *Kindness*: A good heart is a quality that everyone should develop. Modern life can be harsh. Social media is cruel and unforgiving to some people, so showing your kind side will make women melt. Show her you can be a sucker for animals and kids, and you will soon be reaping the benefits!

- *Faithfulness*: No matter what your status, women will not forgive unfaithful men. You can be the bad boy who sleeps with them and discards them, but you should never cheat on them. There is an attractiveness attached to bad boys, but there is no glory in cheating.

- *Great lover*: How you act in bed is just as important as how you act outside of the bedroom. Show her you are not on a solo mission to orgasm! Take care of her needs and make the experience better for both of you. You can always learn more about becoming a better lover, so do your research. It will pay off!

- *Helpfulness*: Alpha males are responsible for all the members of their tribe. The old, the young, and especially the weak. Show you are a true alpha by lending a hand whenever possible. If you see an old lady struggling with shopping, then you should go out of your way to assist her.

- *Economically responsible*: You don't have to be rich or even wealthy to qualify as an alpha male. You do have to show that you understand the need to manage money, though, and make it work for you. Women are looking for someone to provide stability, so they need you to be responsible. This applies to all women, especially if they have successful well-paid careers.

- *Good grooming*: Looking good should not be a chore. You will automatically be judged on first appearances, so make sure they are great. Your clothes are an obvious way to look good, but you can miss the smaller details. Nails and hair should also be clean, tidy, and practical. Have a regular manicure, and show the ladies you understand all about personal grooming.

- *Moral character*: You should be an example to others. Setting standards is part of your alpha role. You should understand that morals matter just as much today as they ever did. Morality is not a dirty word; morality is cool!

- *Make her feel wanted*: You need to convince her you are the real deal before she decides to give herself completely. Be there when she needs you, no matter what. Physically, emotionally and mentally. If she needs your help, then you should give it unconditionally. This is not a show of weakness; it is a strength.

- *Always strive for better*: Personally, and at work, you should always have goals. Being stuck in a rut will make you seem unambitious. Women gravitate to men who are interested in self-improvement and bettering themselves. You don't have to be the richest guy in the room, or the most powerful. You can be a man who is content with his role but realizes he can also benefit from the promotion. Sometimes overachievers can be off-putting as they have little time for the women in their life. A healthy balance is a way to win her over.

- *Masculinity*: Men who look like men will tick all the right boxes. Yes, some good-looking guys can pull off the slightly more feminine look, but not you! You look like a man, you smell like a man (in a good way), and you act like a man. You have short, well-groomed hair, and your nails are also short but beautifully kept. Men look good in suits, men look good in jeans, but they do not look good in ill-fitting clothing!

- *Intelligence*: A quick wit and a healthy sense of fun are attractive in a man. Intelligence can be improved by using different methods. Keep up with news and current affairs by reading online articles. Watch the news and listen to all sides of the arguments. When you are in a company, the best way to shine is to participate in conversations and know what you are talking about. People have never lived in an age where information is as readily available as it is now. There is no excuse for ignorance, so don't show yours!

- *Forgiveness*: A strong man knows the benefits of forgiveness. Choose your battles wisely and show your compassion. If someone has pranged your car, then don't lose it and act like a jerk. Accidents happen and showing your softer side will make you look like the bigger guy. You should only lose your temper when it is really necessary, and then it should still be controlled. If someone poses a threat to your nearest and dearest, then you are entitled to take action. The main thing to remember is always to keep your cool and show you have self-control.

You want to attract classy women. They value themselves and look for the same qualities in men. Resist the temptation to view women who are picky as prudes. They are quite the opposite. They have values that won't be distracted by flashy cars and material wealth.

What are the Qualities That Make Men Unattractive?

An unhealthy pale appearance and dark circles under the eyes.

When you lose sleep, it takes its toll on your appearance. Sleep deprivation makes you look ill. Dark circles and red eyes may make you look like an extra from the latest vampire movie, but it won't attract the ladies!

Mean Behavior

If everyone believed the movies, then it would seem that the mean guys get the women. Good guys tend to come last in fantasy land, but what about the real world? Studies have shown that most people are turned off by expressions of meanness and evil looks. This also applies to online activity. Being cheeky and flirtatious is good, but insulting people and putting them down is an unattractive quality.

Stressful Behavior

Women are looking for someone to take charge. They want a calm, authoritative person who will stand up for them when needed. If you are constantly battling with stress, you will appear less attractive. Try chilling out; it will make you seem healthier and more productive.

Losing Control

This book has already touched on the need to keep control of your temper, but this should apply to other areas as well. Drinking heavily and acting like an idiot is a sure way to make women turn away! Yes, it is okay to have a drink – being sociable is an asset –, but know your limits! If you know you are a lightweight drinker, then steer away from it when you are looking to attract women. Keep the drunken antics for your bros!

There is no need to take it to the extreme. In fact, in recent studies, occasional drinkers were listed as more attractive than non-drinkers. It is all about willpower.

Smoking is also a big no-no in these ultra-healthy times. A man who enjoys a cigar when celebrating is tolerated, but chain smokers are not. They lack discipline, and they smell like ashtrays! Drugs are also not attractive, as women want a clean, healthy man to share their bed.

Laziness

When you are lazy, you are showing disinterest in life and a poor attitude. You are content to drift along without ambition. Women do not want to be the ones who are the driving force behind their men.

They may have an equal role, but they expect enthusiasm and initiative. Get yourself into gear and be the man who is there for other people. You have the energy, just utilize it!

Political Extremes

You may think that your political preferences have no bearing on your love life, and most of the time, that is true. However, you can turn women off if you push your opinions. Have a heated debate, sure, but you also need to understand there are always at least two sides to every story. If you believe passionately in a certain party, then try socializing with like-minded people. Seek out gatherings and meetings of people who have the same political persuasions and see if your perfect women are there!

Being attractive to the opposite sex is important, but so is remaining true to yourself. Never change the core elements that make up your personality. This will only create a fake version of yourself that no one will be happy with. Morals, character, and intelligence are essential, but so is a strong sense of who you are. Follow these guidelines and develop the best version of yourself.

The Alpha Male Personality

In the 21st century, it can be easy to dismiss the concept of the alpha male as old fashioned and outdated. However, the truth is that the alpha male will always have a place in society.

In the animal kingdom, the alpha male is the leader of the group. Every wolf pack and every pride of lions has one. These alphas are responsible for the safety of the group, and they will protect the females and cubs with their lives. These positions are the most important in the group, and the alpha will have to defend their position regularly. Young males will aspire to defeat the alpha male and will challenge him when they feel they are strong enough.

How Has the Term Become Relevant in Human Society?

It is inbuilt in one's psyche to define authority. People look for leaders to follow at school, in college, in the workplace, and while playing sports. Some people are natural leaders and assume positions with ease. Others need to develop their skills and fight to rise through the ranks.

In dating terms, the alpha male will always attract the hottest women. Shy sensitive guys have their place in society, and that is fine – they can date those women who find that attractive. Alpha males are not really attracted to the good girl next door types anyway. They want a woman who is fiery, passionate, wild, and not a wallflower. Alpha males should attract alpha females, and together they will become a power couple!

What are the Traits of a Typical Alpha Male?

1) *They know exactly how attractive they are.* They may look like a male model, or they may just have average looks – it doesn't matter. They know that their masculinity and confidence make them stand out from the crowd.

2) *They are hardworking.* They will work endlessly for their friends and family. Nothing of worth comes easy, and the alpha male understands this.

3) *They are ambitious.* Alpha males don't settle. They have a vision for the future, and it is limitless. Every alpha not only believes in pushing themselves, but they believe in pushing the people who follow them. The alpha male will encourage others to seek success and will help them in any way they can. The alpha male is both a role model and inspiration.

4) *They have a strong masculine vibe.* There is nothing metrosexual about an alpha male. They know that even when they moisturize, take care of their bodily hygiene, and have manicures or pedicures, they are still all men. This is a different time for men, and they can embrace treatments and cosmetics without a hint of femininity.

5) *They are a man's man.* Other men want to be him. They also want to hang out with him and bask in his glory. Other men know that if they are associated with the alpha male, then women will view them more favorably.

6) *They can change and adapt to the culture.* Alpha males know that the status quo is always changing. Women are looking for men who are not stuck in the past. The alpha male will never stop learning because life never stops teaching.

7) *They know how to deal with stress.* Alpha males will be subject to stress. That is a fact that can't be ignored, but they also know how to deal with it. They know the power of meditation and relaxation and are not afraid to use these techniques. There is nothing feminine

about meditation. LeBron James, Steve Jobs, and the whole of the Seattle Seahawks have used meditation to relieve stress.

8) *Expect respect.* Most guys want to be liked; they want a woman to like them and become their friend. Alpha males demand respect; the friendship can come later. His very demeanor demands the respect of everyone he meets.

9) *He has self-respect.* If you want others to respect you, then you need to respect yourself first. Alpha males believe in themselves and back every decision they make. If they decide they are interested in a woman, they believe they will succeed in their seduction.

10) *They learn from failure.* It would be a mistake to think that alpha males never fail. They are, after all, humans. The difference is that they never give up; their enthusiasm drives them onward to success.

11) They *understand communication.* Alpha males are meant to be heard. They know that this doesn't necessarily mean their words need to be powerful. They know that their tone and body language also play a major part in getting their message across.

12) *They understand image.* Alpha males will never be caught looking less than their best. Even in sweats and gym gear, they look amazing. How you dress is a way of communicating who you are without saying a word. Alpha males will have a classy, understated wardrobe that fits their bodies like a glove. They will wear an outfit well, from their shoes to their head; they will scream elegance.

13) *They are rulebreakers.* Alpha males think outside the box. They are fearless enough to recognize that the only way to progress is to challenge society. Rules do not apply to alphas, but they will only break them when the occasion calls for it.

14) *They know how to flirt.* The art of flirting is one of an alpha male's greatest gifts. They can make a woman think they are the only person in the room. They are not overtly sexual; they treat women with respect. They do, however, have the confidence to talk to a lady with the knowledge they won't be rejected. They love talking to women and are totally at ease in female company.

15) *They are strong.* Physical strength is important, obviously, but mental toughness is also paramount. Willpower, optimism, resistance to authority, and ambition power their every thought.

Alpha males have evolved through the ages. The modern alpha male is the most advanced version of the species. The myths that surround alpha males still exist and need to be dealt with.

Dealing with Myths and Replacing Them with Truths

Myth: *All alpha males are thugs.* If the only source of information people had were films and television, then you would probably come to the same conclusion. They are portrayed as the muscle-bound thug who beats up all the other guys. They are tough and unapproachable, but women still fall at their feet

Truth: *Alpha males are generally good guys.* They are born leaders who inspire their pack to succeed. They want other people to be happy, and their feelings are often based on love and compassion.

There are bad boy alphas who walk all over other people to get what they want. Women may be initially attracted to this type of behavior, but they will soon see through this thuggish behavior. Selfish jerks may look like alphas, but they fail to act like them.

Good guy alphas have a toughness, but they understand what compassion is and when to use it. Think about alpha males who have changed the world. They are revolutionaries who do not bully.

Myth: *Alphas are born not made.* Yes, some alphas are born leaders and have been assigned their position by society. Think of princes and kings who have been alpha males. They are born into their position and thrust into leadership.

Truth: *Most alphas are created by hard work.* You may not have been born into a privileged position, but you can still rise to the top with hard work and perseverance. You can develop skills and traits that will make you an alpha male.

Myth: *You must be tall to be an alpha.* The image of a man striding into a room, head and shoulders above the crowd, conjures up an image of the classic alpha male. You can't be short and attract the ladies, or can you?

Truth: *There are plenty of alpha males who are classed as short.* If you are vertically challenged, should you restrict your female companions to ones who are shorter than you? Hell, no, you shouldn't! Wear your height with pride! Pursue those leggy lovelies and know that your confidence and personality will give you as much chance as the six-foot-plus guys. Don't believe that short alphas exist? Check out this list!

Floyd Mayweather, Jr: Height 5'8". Also known as Money Mayweather. He runs with a crew that he calls the "Money Team." He is surrounded by friends, family, and amazing women wherever he goes. What he says goes! He also has a savvy head for business, as well as being a successful boxer.

Tom Cruise: Height 5'7". Is there anyone on Earth who would argue that Tom is not an alpha male? He has been seen with some of the most beautiful women in the world, even those who dwarf him. He has commanded roles that should not have been played by short men – Jack Reacher, to name but one. His height is inconsequential to his success.

Vladimir Putin: Height 5'7". Yes, Putin is not always a good guy, but no one can argue he is not an alpha male. He rides through forests on horseback with his chest bare and his masculinity for all to see. The Russian people will follow him to the ends of the world and are loyal to him. His dating history is remarkable – even Pamela Anderson is reported to have fallen for his charms.

Kevin Hart: Height 5'2". Comedian, actor, producer, and all-round successful guy, Hart is worth over $200 million. His inclusion on this list may be contentious, but he deserves mention just for his success with the ladies. The comedian does seem to have a liking for statuesque ladies. He has also successfully published his own rules for success – a very alpha male thing to do.

Myth: *Alpha males are flashy and surrounded by material wealth.* Once again, the movies and television govern how people perceive alpha males. The loud guy with the Porsche and the bling will often be seen getting the girl. They will be seen as the top dog and alpha male.

Truth: Some women are attracted by material wealth and possessions, but they will prove to be shallow. Real women are attracted by the inner man. The qualities of an alpha male come mostly from within. Charisma, energy, confidence, and enthusiasm will soon eclipse a flashy car and a bulging bank balance.

If you do not believe this fact, just think about the definition of a gold digger. The women who attach themselves to wealthy flashy men, marry them, wait five years, and then divorce them for 50 percent of their worth.

Myth: *Alpha males mistreat women.* Probably the biggest misconception around. Once again, movies and television have portrayed the idea that the "treat them mean and keep them keen" attitude works.

Truth: *Nice guys can be alphas.* When a woman rejects a nice guy, it is because they have become boring. Alpha guys treat their ladies like queens, but they also know how to keep them interested. Alphas may have some bad boy attitude, but they will never mistreat women. Attitude is attractive when used positively.

Myth: *Alpha males are a concept that doesn't exist.* This idea has been crafted by men who have no idea how to become an alpha. They acknowledge that strong personalities and passion are successful, but the whole notion of an alpha male belongs in the animal kingdom.

Truth: *Of course alpha males exist.* They have existed since the dawn of time. If alpha males did not take charge and inspire their followers, the world would have ground to a halt. Alpha males have also influenced history, some in positive ways, and others in ways that are probably better forgotten! Some would argue that Hitler, Mussolini, and Obama bin Laden were alpha males. This is true, but as far as seduction goes, you are talking about less violent aspects of the alpha personality!

Strategy 1: Confidence

What is Confidence?

Men know that confidence is a huge attraction for women. Where do these confident men get their skills from? Are they born with this amazing self-belief, or did they get it from success? Many strategies out there can give you intermittent confidence and may even lead to a few dates.

An alpha male shuns this type of strategy. He is looking for a level of confidence that he knows will win the ladies over. If you suffer from low self-confidence, you will struggle to talk to attractive women. Do you stumble over your words and end up running in the opposite direction because you fear that every woman will see through your façade and discover your innermost insecurities? Well, that ends now!

Nobody is born with confidence; it is a mindset that requires work. Are you prepared to put that work in? Of course you are, so time to get going!

Exercise One: *Your winning smile.*

You need to have a smile that is confident, welcoming, and approachable. You really do not want to come across as a grinning fool. Think gentle laughter rather than guffawing! Here is how to develop the perfect smile.

- Stand in front of a full-length mirror and recall something amusing, maybe a good joke or funny situation.
- React to it. Laugh gently while relaxing your face. You may have to fake it at first, and that's okay. The exercise is all about observing how natural you look.
- Change the laughter into a smile. Raise one side of your mouth to give a lop-sided look to your smile, a cheeky grin that shows your sense of fun.
- Check the mirror. Is the rest of your face smiling as well? Are the corners of your eyes crinkled? Are your cheeks pulled up?
- Then let the smile fade until your face has a natural, relaxed expression.
- Repeat the exercise until you are comfortable with the feeling.

You can now use your winning smile to impress the next woman you are talking to.

Exercise Two: *Destroy the anxiety associated with approaching women.*

- Use the same full-length mirror to observe yourself.
- Imagine you have spotted a beautiful woman you want to talk to.
- Nod in her direction and turn on that winning smile.
- As soon as you have done the nod, start walking in her direction.
- Walk with confidence and a comfortable stride.
- Once you have reached the imaginary woman, begin to speak.

This exercise is designed to stop you from hesitating. Women know when you have noticed them, and any hesitation on your part will give them the impression that you are not self-confident. Even if they are not initially interested, they will be intrigued to meet this super confident guy.

Exercise Three: *Use your confidence as a shield.*

Have you ever been subjected to criticism that has left its mark? As in, not constructive criticism, but nasty, unhelpful, and downright insulting comments that are designed to make you feel bad? Try this exercise to help you deal with petty, jealous people who just want to put you down.

- Take a pen and piece of paper.
- Recall all the insults and derogatory comments that have affected you. Go back as far as school and as recent as last week.
- List the people who made the comments and what you recall about them.
- With your increased level of confidence, how would you reply to the hurtful comments today?
- Where are the people who made the comments now? Are they successful and happy?

Understanding why these people made the comments they did is the key. You now know that the comments say more about them than they do about you. They lacked confidence in their own abilities and were trying to bring you down to their level. There is only one person responsible for how you think about yourself – you!

Exercise Four: *The three-compliment journal.*

This exercise is all about encouraging self-love. How are you going to win the love of a good woman if you do not love yourself?

- Take a blank journal and pen.
- When you wake in the morning, grab the journal, and write down three compliments to yourself.
- Maybe you like the way your hair looks in the morning or the way your eyes sparkle.
- Write down one aspect of your personality that you love – your intelligence or humor, perhaps?
- Now read the compliments back to yourself and congratulate yourself on these points.
- Repeat daily until you exhaust all your good points.

You may feel a little self-conscious at first, but this exercise is powerful. Think of yourself as an empty barrel that you are filling drop by drop. The first day you may not even notice the difference; even after the first week, there may be no change. However, one day you will wake up, and your self-confidence barrel will be full to the brim!

Exercise Five: *Make a self-esteem collage.*

Visual aids are a great way to remind yourself what your dreams and aspirations are. Modern homes are often decorated with inspiring mantras that take the form of art. You can benefit from these types of art, or you can make your own. Take a whiteboard and place pictures of the dream destination of your perfect holiday. Use images of the things you desire, that inspire confidence, and raise expectations. Browse through magazines to find these images. This exercise will help you remember who you are, what you are capable of, and what you are entitled to because you deserve it.

Exercise Six: *Treat yourself to something nice.*

When you are suffering from low self-esteem, you can believe you are not worthy of anything good. Why should you treat yourself if you have done nothing to deserve it? A great way to change that perception is to believe you are worthy of appreciation.

Do you love a spa session? A hot stone massage followed by a steam room? Well, book yourself into a local spa center and indulge yourself. It need not be an expensive treat; it is the gesture that counts. Do something nice for yourself and make yourself feel better, as your self-esteem will rise along with your confidence levels.

Exercise Seven: *Make a difference to others.*

Volunteering is a great way to improve self-confidence. Join a local group that aims to help people who are less fortunate and learn how you can make a difference. There is nothing more humbling than interacting with people who are facing serious dilemmas in life. You will feel better about yourself, and you will feel like a worthier individual as you help others. Food kitchens are a great way to meet new people and make a significant contribution to your neighborhood.

Exercise Eight: *Pursue a dream.*

Finding a hobby that fills you with passion can make your self-esteem go through the roof. Is there anything that you always wanted to do but felt you lacked the skills? Have you ever thought you could be a wildlife photographer or play an instrument? What has held you back in the past? A lack of self-belief can be a hard barrier to overcome. Check out local courses and see if they have anything that appeals to you. Join Facebook groups who have the same passions as you. Imagine the pride you will feel when you take that first step on the path to success. Now imagine that feeling as you prepare to approach a beautiful woman that you previously would have thought was out of your league. Satisfying, right?

These eight techniques will help you improve your self-confidence, but there are times when you will feel yourself slip back into low self-esteem. You need a positive focus group to help you get back on track. Think about it; everyone needs support at certain points in their life.

Creating a Focus Group

Organize your friends and family into a group that can be called upon to help when times get tough. Choose people who know you well and are known for their honesty. This is your support network, and they can be a powerful tool to boost your confidence. Once the group has been organized, use the time together to focus on one person at a time. The rest of the group will speak individually and talk about the things they like about the person who has been identified.

Once everyone has spoken, choose another individual to focus on and repeat the exercise. This carries on until every person in the group has been a positive focus. You may feel this technique is a little bit off the wall, but it is just friends backing up other friends. No one is suggesting you meet in a meadow and all wear flowing robes. You can meet in a bar or a coffee shop and just have normal conversations as well as positive affirmations. The idea is to boost each other and know you have a support group, should you need it.

Strategy 2: Physique and Image

Both the male and female brains are hardwired to make assumptions based on body types. Women are looking for a body that is designed to give them the perfect offspring they desire. Thus, a virile, healthy, and strong physique will have the ladies queueing up to date you.

What is an Alpha Male Physique?

Forget the atypical idea of bodybuilders glistening with sweat. Superheroes are called that because that is what they are, and women appreciate that. Professional athletes are also generally unattainable, but all these men have an underlying body type that resembles a walking billboard of virility.

Broad shoulders that taper down to a narrow waist accompanied by strong calves all signify an alpha male physique. So, how do you develop this type of physique? With work and dedication.

A healthy physique begins with a healthy diet, so here are a few tips to get you started on your alpha physique.

The master plan to create a better, faster, stronger, and manlier you begins with the fuel you put into your body. Do you know what your body needs to lose fat and gain muscle? You probably do – protein builds muscle and keeps you full. Fact.

Protein is used by the body to repair damaged muscle, bone, and teeth; it is the mortar that keeps the body whole. Here are the best sources of protein available:

- Fish and seafood
- White meat (chicken, turkey, and duck_
- Beef (stick to lean cuts like tenderloin and sirloin steaks)
- Low-fat dairy products (like yogurt, milk, and cheese)
- Eggs
- Pork (lean cuts only)
- Pulses, beans, and lentils

Combined with a diet rich in good fats (sunflower oil, salmon, avocados, and all omega-3 sources), healthy carbs (vegetables, fruit, potatoes, and legumes), and no processed foods will soon have you on the road to an alpha physique.

Developing your Alpha Physique

Now that you have your diet in place, it is time to exercise. Begin with the upper torso and develop those broad shoulders and pumped arms.

Broad shoulders give off signals to both men and women. You are telling other men that you are a force to be reckoned with, and they should think twice before challenging you. Women will also pick up on the same signals and feel safe in your company.

Exercises that Improve the Shoulders

Standing press. This is a great mass builder for the whole body. Stand with your feet apart and raise the dumbbell into the air for 15 reps. Change arms and repeat.

Seated dumbbell press. Sit on a bench and grab a pair of dumbbells. Raise them nice and high then lower them to the floor. Being seated helps you isolate the shoulder motion.

Lateral raise. Grab some light dumbbells and hold them next to your sides with bent elbows. Place your feet shoulder-width apart and squeeze your core. Raise your arms to form the letter T, pause for a beat, and then lower.

Pumped Arms

The trick to having pumped arms is they should be big but still functional. You do not want to look like the Hulk bursting out of your sleeves. Your arms signify your hunting prowess and trigger the female brain to recognize the signs of a good provider.

The exercises listed below are easy to do and perfect for beginners. Once mastered, you can progress to more intense exercises.

Press-ups: These will target your arms, shoulders, and chest. Place your hands flat on the floor and extend your arms. Your legs should be extended and your knees off the floor. Form a plank from head to toe. Lower yourself as far as possible, hold the position, and then raise to the original position. Repeat for up to 50 reps.

Wall push-ups: Targets triceps. Stand at arm's length from the wall. Place the palms of your hands on the wall at shoulder height. Tuck elbows in and bends your arms to lower yourself towards the wall. Raise your heels and stand on tiptoe as you approach the wall. Your body should always remain plank-like. If you want to intensify the exercise, stand further away from the wall and lower your hands. Repeat up to 20 times.

Bench dips: Targets triceps. Take a chair and place it behind you. Put the heel of your hands on the seat part and grip the edges. Lower yourself to the floor while keeping your knees at a 90-degree angle. Repeat up to 20 times.

You can also use your barbells and dumbbells to do curls.

Waist

You are not striving to have a waist that looks like a ballerina or a Victorian woman. That would look ridiculous. You are simply ridding your midsection of excess fat. A smaller waist shows you are in shape, healthy, and ready for action.

Try these exercises for a smaller waist.

Figure Eights: Lie on the floor with straight legs raised in the air. Create sweeping arcs with your legs that resemble the figure eight. Allow your hips to roll with the movement and get creative with your movement. This is a deep hit for your core and helps strengthen your lower back. Try a variation and mimic the action of a windshield wiper with your legs.

Burpees: These are effective fat burning exercises that can be done anywhere and without equipment. Crouch on your toes with your hands flat on the floor. Jump up and propel your legs backward until they are fully extended. Bring your legs back to their original position. Jump up and raise your arms into the air. Repeat 20 times.

Side plank: Simply put, one of the best exercises for developing core muscles. Place your right arm on the floor, supporting your weight with your elbow and lower arm. Your right ankle and foot should remain on the ground while the rest of your body forms a rigid plank. Hold the position for two minutes and then change position, so your left side is doing all the work.

Calves

These are the most stubborn part of the body to develop. Everyone knows someone who has great claves yet does nothing to deserve them! Why are calves important? Men need to tell the ladies that they have endurance, strength, and staying power – and big calves will do that.

Calf strengthening exercises.

Double leg calf raises: Stand near a wall and place your feet shoulder-width apart. Using the wall for balance, press down the balls of your feet to raise your body. Hold your abdominal muscles in and maintain a straight upward movement.

You can add variations to this move by standing on a stair to increase the intensity. You can also add weights to make the exercise more intense.

Standing calf raise: Create an elevated surface like a step or low bench. Stand with the ball of your left foot on the elevated surface and place your right toes on the left ankle. Tighten your core and raise your left heel as far as possible. Begin to lower the left heel until you feel the calf muscle stretch. Repeat with alternate legs for up to 20 reps.

You can also use weights to make this exercise more intense.

Farmers walk on toes: This is a variation on the traditional exercise that is excellent for strengthening calf muscles. Hold a dumbbell in each hand and place feet shoulder length apart. Lower your shoulders and stand on your tiptoes. Walk forward for 15 steps, and reverse until you are in the original position. Repeat five times.

Your calves can also benefit from traditional exercises like walking, jump rope, and skipping. These exercises are designed to be easily accessible and can be performed without joining a gym. However, if you do want to become a more improved specimen, then physical trainers can help you work on problem areas.

There is not much you can do about your height or body type, but you can make the best of the gifts nature gave you. You can become a pocket rocket or a well-toned tall guy – just remember that it is all about giving off the right signals.

The alpha male is all about confidence, and as you develop your torso, you will also feel more self-confident. The whole image is about looking the best you can without coming across as unapproachable.

Women are looking for men who are genetically perfected to meet their needs. And women know exactly what they want. They want a warrior to protect them, a hunter to provide for them, and a stud to satisfy their needs in the bedroom. You will signal your ability to meet these needs with your physique and image.

Strategy 3: Body Language

The alpha male has two main aims. He needs to show women that he is the real deal, the best of the species, and the prime example of what a man should be. He also needs to show other males that they should back off and try their luck elsewhere.

Modern alphas know that they need to be the whole package. They project an expectation with their appearance, and they need to back it up with appropriate body language.

First, Consider your Posture

Good posture is essential for an alpha male. If you slouch or stand with your shoulders slumped, you look like you are uninterested. Standing straight with your shoulders back projects your personality. You look like a man with a mission, and this inspires those around you. When you find yourself slouching, imagine there is a string at the top of your head and pull it! Relax your shoulders and arms, lift your chin, and straighten your spine. Now you are ready to slay the ladies with your killer body language!

Walk the walk: Alpha males know exactly where they need to be and when they need to be there. Consider nervous men. They are hesitant and jumpy, and this shows in their pace. They are desperate to get to their destination and prone to hurried, frantic types of steps. Now contrast that with the alpha male walk of confidence. They are unhurried, calm, and measured. They take the time to survey their environment and take in all the details.

Now no one is suggesting you walk at a snail's pace, as that is not an attractive look. The key is to walk with purpose but without unneeded haste. Never keep people waiting but learn how to adjust your speed to match others, especially girls. No woman wants to be scurrying after a man, as it is just demeaning.

Sit like an alpha: Have you ever noticed how men sit in public? Some sit with their shoulders slumped, hunched over, their head down, and totally engrossed with the floor. Others sit with their legs splayed out and their crown jewels on show. Both positions are familiar sights but are not the kind of posture that attracts positive female attention.

The modern alpha will take his place on a chair in a comfortable position. He will lean back, cross his legs at the ankle, and may even place one arm behind his neck to show his ease with the situation. He will never break eye contact as he sits, he is open for business, so to speak, and is indicating his willingness to engage.

Have an open stance: Your body language gives out subliminal messages to others about your dominance. You may feel that showing your vulnerability goes against alpha principles, but the opposite is true. A truly confident man will never be afraid to show their vulnerability, and the ladies love this! When you are talking to someone, try putting your arms and hands behind your back. You are opening your chest and subconsciously showing people that you are afraid of nothing.

Master the shake: Having a proper handshake has often been described as a sign of a real man. Does this just mean that the guy who can squeeze the hardest is then automatically an alpha male? No. There is an art to shaking someone's hand, and it is not all about strength. Take the hand firmly, shake for no more than three times, and then release. Accompany the shake with a friendly smile and always say something.

Understanding when to touch a woman: The ultimate exercise in connecting with a woman is knowing when it is appropriate to use touch. When it is done right, touch is the ultimate demonstration of the alpha that wishes to engage. Most women know when a guy is creepily touching them and will have no problem telling them so. Alpha males know the boundaries and will never stray outside of them. Try a hug when you meet a new lady, and after that, mirror her touch. If she places her hand on your arm, she is signaling to you that you may engage in the same way.

Display your strength: You already know the advantages of looking strong. Women will recognize the attraction of your broad shoulders and pumped arms, but how can you build on this impression. The best way is to use the strength you have so carefully nurtured. If someone needs something moving, make sure you lend a hand. If you see a lady struggling with shopping or other heavy goods, then offer to carry them for her. Displaying your physical strength is a real turn on for women, so why would you pass up the opportunity to do it?

Understanding the Gestures that Single You Out as an Alpha Male

You now know how to stand, sit, and make a great first impression. You now need to understand how to maintain that impression. Gestures are a subtle way to convey your position and signal your alpha status.

Steepling

Raise your hands toward your chest or face, then gently bring your fingertips together and press. This gesture is one that indicates you are considering your options with inner confidence. It implies you have the situation in hand. You are confident and even superior. This gesture is one of assertiveness without displaying aggression.

Use your Smile Sparingly

You know the power of your smile. It makes people feel comfortable and welcome when you meet them for the first time. It signals your love of life and your sense of fun. However, if you overuse your smile, it can lose potency. Think of alphas in the media and their "normal" expressions. They will look like the badass guys they are. Mean and moody can also look hot and sexy. When you do use your smile, it can be as deadly as an arrow to the heart!

Putting it all Together

Your body language is always speaking. Non-verbal communication makes up a huge proportion of how people communicate. The tips above will communicate to the world that you are an alpha male who deserves respect, attention, and interaction. But what is the secret to making the women you want respond every time?

This statement may shock you, but it will also make you want to try it out. The trick to coming across as confident, sexy, and impossible to resist is to be non-reactive!

Just think about it. What do men desire the most? Anything they cannot have! So, try this simple exercise next time you are in the company of a drop-dead gorgeous gal.

Imagine: You have met a woman who definitely gets your juices flowing. You are with company and just happen to be facing away from her when she calls your name. You respond immediately, right? Wrong. You wait a couple of seconds, then turn your head slowly and give her your killer gaze. Speak in a slow, steady voice and ask her if she needs you. Only when she answers in the positive, do you turn your body towards her. Slowly make your way to her side and then engage.

Handy tip: As you walk toward the woman in question, make sure you make sharp eye contact with any other attractive women in your eye line.

Trying to become non-reactive can be difficult. It goes against every natural reaction you possess. However, if you can force yourself to adopt this technique, you will see a dramatic shift in the way women respond to you.

They will be intrigued by you. Do not forget that naturally beautiful women are used to men who respond to their every whim. They are not used to waiting for a response. They will want to find out more about the guy who seems interested but not overly eager. They will go out of their way to include you in conversations as you are an enigma wrapped up in a good-looking package!

Developing your sexy, attractive, confident body language is a key way to make the world your oyster. Women will drop at your feet, and men will marvel at your appeal. You are the alpha, and you know how to behave like one!

Strategy 4: Frame Control

Frame control is all about persuasion and communication. You will paint a picture with your words that not only speaks to you but everyone else in the conversation. When used for seduction, it is not just saying nice things to make a girl like you. It also isn't about being unreactive to make her chase you.

Having a strong frame is one of the most important things you can do when you are developing your alpha persona. It is a form of verbal chess that involves planning and looking for opportunities to score a point.

The best way to develop your strong frame is through experience. You must have had conversations when you have been dismissed or merely ignored by a woman because your reply was weak. In hindsight, have you thought, "If only I had said (such and such) I could have prolonged the conversation and won her round to my way of thinking?" Well, that is a lesson well learned.

You develop your frame by subjecting yourself to pressure. If you are hoping to win over women with your frame, then you need to develop your frame. This can involve changing your focus when you talk to women. Originally your need to get her to sleep with you was your primary objective, but what if you changed this objective and based the whole experience on personal development.

Adopting this mindset will help you in two ways. First, you are removing the internal pressure to be successful at getting laid as that is not your number one objective. You are on a quest to make yourself a better man. You want to guide conversations to your advantage. You want to put yourself in social interactions that make you uncomfortable so you can overcome the weak areas in your frame.

The best way to illustrate what a strong frame looks like is to give examples.

You have spotted a girl you think is attractive across the bar. You know her slightly, so you approach her with the following dialogue.

You: "Hi, how are you? It's great to see you again. Are you with friends?"

Her: "Hi, I'm great, thanks. Yes, I'm with a group of friends who are around somewhere."

You: "How nice. I'm just having a drink with a buddy as well. Listen, do you fancy meeting up for a drink later in the week?"

Her: "That would be great, but it's only as friends, right?"

You: "Of course, that would be lovely. I'll give you a ring later and arrange it."

You have shown your weak frame and instantly been diminished to the friend zone. It is very difficult to get out of the friend zone, so what should you have done differently?

Your last line should have been along these lines.

You: "Okay, I'll take that, but I'm guessing we'll have so much fun that you'll soon want to upgrade me to dating material."

You will have made her think twice about you. Your confidence and self-belief, combined with a strong frame, have her thinking differently about a simple drinks date.

When you enter a conversation confident of success, you will see a clearer picture than a less confident person. You will see the different ways to steer the subject into your comfort zone.

Frame Control Exercises

Have you always had more success with women who are standing alone, maybe at a party or a bar? Do you avoid groups of women as you feel they are intimidating? Change those perceptions and tackle your fears. Once you have spotted a group of attractive women, decide which one you are going to talk to and then make your move. Frame your conversation to show just exactly what you expect from the encounter. If you approach her with confidence, you won't care what the reaction of her friends is. This woman needs to see you as a potential date, and your whole persona should be dedicated to getting her to see you that way.

How to Communicate What You Want

Have you ever asked a girl to dance and been rejected? Why did you ask her to dance in the first place? Do you like dancing? Did you want to move things along with her by asking her to dance? Did you think she looked like she wanted to dance? It could have been any one of these and a dozen other reasons. How is she supposed to know why you asked her?

Framing helps you communicate with her what you want. Know what you want and identify the "why: behind your request. Try phrases like the following:

- "Wow, it's noisy here. Let's find somewhere quieter so we can chat. I'd love to get to know you better."
- "Come with me. I know a much better place than this for music. You'll love the resident band they have."
- "Why don't we go out next week with your friend and her boyfriend? He is such good company, and we would have a great time."

Once you explain that you promise a positive and enjoyable experience, there is a greater chance that she will agree.

The Next Step

If a girl does resist, this is known as a frame encounter. Now you have a decision to make. Do you persist to the bitter end, or do you walk away after the first negative encounter? What you do not do is halfway persist. If you ask a couple of times and then back down, you have allowed the balance of power to shift. She has outframed you and will never see you as an alpha male. She may agree to a pity date further down the line but will never have any real romantic notions about you.

If you have asked once and get the idea that she is about to reject you, then just shrug and find another girl to focus on. If you can manage to do this right in the middle of her decline, then you have shown her what she is missing. If there is not anyone else to distract your attention, try cutting her off by changing the subject completely. The idea is to leave her on the back foot, wondering what just happened. Why aren't you devastated and crushed by her rejection? Her interest is now piqued!

Or you can take the stance that you will keep asking until she says yes. Now, you might think this makes you seem desperate, but if you frame it right, it can be endearing. Try something like this.

You: "Hey, I'm going to grab a coffee. Do you want to join me?"

Her: "I don't drink coffee. I think..."

You: "No worries. They do a tasty herbal tea that is really healthy."

Her: "I'm okay here, thanks. I don't really need a drink."

You: "You'll enjoy yourself once we get there. I really think you'll enjoy the place. Come on."

This type of persistence will be seen as cute, and not many women will be able to resist such an interesting approach. Of course, if you sense that the whole thing is becoming a lost cause, then you should back off immediately. You should not be interested in anyone who has zero interest in you.

Should the lady in question comply and decide to join you, then you need to reward her. You should never bring up the frame encounter even though you are feeling great about it. Basking in your own success is not a good look! Instead, you should make her feel good about her choice. Reward her with some strong emotional connections. Be sure to show her affection with your physical closeness. She has decided to trust you and take the relationship forward, and you need to show her you recognize the chance she has taken.

You need to avoid any girl asking the question, "What's the point?" when you suggest an activity. Nobody wants to feel they are wasting their time with other people, and therefore you need to state your intentions from the outset. Remember: Women will often test your resolve and challenge your sense of authority. You are the alpha; use your skills to show them that if you believe they are worth pursuing, then you are quite willing to either walk away or pursue them until they comply.

Strategy 5: Natural Leadership

As stated, women rely on their primal instincts when choosing a man. In a tribe, the natural leader would have his pick of the womenfolk. His strengths would appeal to them in three different ways. They know that he is the strongest in times of conflict, the smartest in times of trouble, and the kindest in times of tranquility.

Consider the saying, "Men want a lady in the living room, a chef in the kitchen, and a tiger in the bedroom." Well, flip that around. Women want a hunter in the forest, a king in the village, and a lover in the bedroom.

Of course, modern men are more evolved. They have multiple skills that appeal to women. The alpha male will be a larger than life character, the best at what he does, and have a reputation as a man who knows how to please a lady – both inside and outside of the bedroom.

Here are Some Traits of the Modern Alpha Male

- *He prefers to have the final word*: His confidence is such that he believes his opinion is supremely relevant. He will listen to others, but mostly, he will have something to add.

- *He has the confidence to make friends with other alpha males*: He doesn't fear other alphas; he relishes the opportunity to learn from them. Kings are quite happy to make friends with other kings.

He will also relish the thought of competition. How will he know his limits if they are never tested?

- *He appreciates talent:* He knows that he is the leader of his tribe. Yet, he also knows that delegation is the key to a successful community. The modern alpha is no different. They promote other people with talent and recognize their input is important.

- *He can be blunt:* He will not be rude or arrogant; he simply doesn't mince his words. Why use 20 words when just two will get the same message across? Time is important to an alpha, and you will rarely see him wasting it, especially in pointless conversation.

- *He accepts constructive criticism:* A leader is always learning.

- *He moves on from negative situations:* He won't forget what has happened, but he refuses to dwell. Ordinary people dwell on the past; alpha males are all about the future.

- *He will encourage rather than direct:* He knows how to issue orders, but he also realizes that not everyone responds well to directions. Instead, he encourages people to excel; he will push them to achieve things rather than telling them to do it.

- *He is a dreamer and a doer:* While this may seem like an oxymoron, natural leaders dare to dream. They also believe that their dreams are infinitely doable. This is a form of inspiration that can't be beaten. When someone sees a dream become a reality, it drives them onward to greater heights.

- *He will empower rather than reward:* When you are given a reward for successful action, the joy you feel will be fleeting. If you are promoted or empowered, the feeling is lasting. A natural leader understands this because he understands the joy of empowerment himself.

- *He outworks everyone:* Natural leaders should be prepared to work tirelessly and take on every role. He will live by the mantra, "Never ask anyone to do something you aren't prepared to do yourself."

- *He sets the tone:* An alpha male will enter a room and determine the mood in seconds. If he is in the mood for fun, then the mood will lighten. If he is feeling industrious, the whole room will be energized. He radiates energy and emotion. And ladies, if he is in the mood for sex, every inch of your body will feel the heat!

● *He is creative*: Natural leaders shun anything bland. He enjoys creativity in others; he encourages ideas that are off the wall and inspiring. His leadership skills push others to succeed; his personal creativity will give successful input.

● *He requires loyalty*: If you betray an alpha male, then you are dead to him. He values his friends and colleagues yet always requires them to show their loyalty. Never go behind his back, never sell him out, and if you are his partner, never cheat on him.

● *He will have a goal-based mentality*: He is always striving to better himself and others around him. He is open to feedback and team responsibility.

● *He welcomes cross-cultural interactions*: Alpha males will embrace cultures that offer an opportunity to learn new skills. He will not be a normal tourist when visiting overseas; he will be the guy who visits the local hotspots and embraces the local color. He will bring back the tastes and experiences he is dying to share with his pack. Your typical alpha male will love to experiment with food and fusion recipes.

● *He will always go first*: Of course he will – he's a leader! Combined with the fact that he is confident of his ability to inspire others, he sees a chance to lead in every activity.

● *He prepares for every scenario*: Natural leaders must prepare for all experiences with military precision. He knows what will happen if someone else fails to deliver. He will have contingency plans and alternative paths to take. Natural leaders will never show panic or weakness; they understand that weak emotions tend to affect others like wildfire.

● *He views conflict as a plus*: If his life was running smoothly and without conflict, he would soon become bored. He thrives on problems and decision making. Life for a natural leader should be exciting and challenging.

- *He will say no if he means no:* Contrary to popular belief, it takes courage to say no. Weaker individuals will say yes just to keep people happy. A natural alpha would rather say no than create expectations they can't fulfill. He will be willing to explore other options, but if an alpha says no to something, chances are it can't be done.

- *He values intangible assets:* Everyone recognizes the tangible assets that signal success. The big house, the latest model car, the expensive wristwatch, and the power wardrobe – to name just a few. However, true alphas understand that real power comes from the assets you can't see or hold. Name recognition, knowledge, and know-how rate highly. Respect and goodwill can't be banked but are invaluable to a successful alpha.

- *He admires inspirational figures and emulates them:* Everyone is aware of impressive people and the roles they play in society. Normal men will look at these figures and feel envy, admiration, and a sense of wonder. Alpha males and natural leaders will view them as role models, people they can learn from, and guys they would love to hang with! They know some revere these figures but they just see them as equals who have gained publicity.

- *He understands relationship leadership:* Alpha males will listen to others and refrain from speaking when the situation dictates. They are great listeners; they know how to focus on others and allow them to shine. Being the loudest person in the room is not always the only indication of leadership.

- *He has a true sense of responsibility:* He will never pass the buck or blame others. If he is willing to take the spoils of success, then he also must assume responsibility when his team fails. That said, he will never walk away from a failure without learning something. A natural leader will always see the positives, even in the most negative situations.

- *He has emotional intelligence:* He is always in control of his emotions. He will never be subject to emotional outbursts. You know if an alpha male displays an emotion, he has considered the effect it will have on others. He is capable of passion, anger, and love, but they will never control him.

- *He doesn't neglect any aspect of his life*: Natural leadership is all about balance. Alpha males know that managing his work life, his personal life, and other responsibilities take work and planning. He will not glibly expect his partner to understand if he must dedicate time to work. Instead, he will make sure that any time spends with them is extra special.

- *He understands the benefit of a deputy*: Leaders can't do everything for everyone all the time. He knows the benefit of a wingman; someone who can take the slack and allow the alpha to take stock is essential. Think about a pride of lions. There is an alpha male who leads, and then there is the beta male who is being prepared for leadership. Society dictates that well-led teams are more effective than solo operations.

There are leaders in all fields. Psychology has long pondered the question, "Are they born or made?" The best estimate seems to be 30 percent born and 70 percent made. This is good news for everyone. Develop the above traits and make yourself a leader of men.

Strategy 6: Purpose

Alpha males have a clear purpose. They are not the sort of men that drift through life, floating from one experience to the next. They understand that purpose is what drives them. They know that having a plan and working to achieve their purpose is what makes them successful.

You are already aware that primal instincts and traditional roles have governed men's behaviors since the dawn of time. Modern men, however, have different goals. They still see themselves as providers, but this can be viewed in a few ways. They now have the opportunity to provide their partners with more freedom by becoming a primary caregiver or being an equal provider within the relationship.

Society has evolved, and now people fill the traditional roles once played by men. Farmers and supermarkets provide food. The police and military provide safety. This enables modern men to decide what they consider to be their true purpose in life without having to consider more traditional roles.

How Will This Help Me Date Hot Women?

Good question! And the answer is that women love a man with a purpose. Alpha males are not seeking permission from anyone to grab life with both hands and live it. They are on a path to success, and they are pursuing their goals with ferocity. This is appealing to women because it gives them a hint of what is to come. Imagine all that energy and purpose channeled into the bedroom! That is why women love a man with a purpose, so what next?

It can be difficult for men to be men in a society that does not require them to be an alpha. The drive and passion for experiencing risk and danger are still there, but they have been filtered down to become secondary. Men still feel the need to protect and provide for their loved ones, but the opportunity to take part in combat opportunities has disappeared.

Some men use video games and on-screen experiences to quell their natural desires while others take part in martial arts. These are all acceptable ways to indulge the need to pit men against men and see what they are made of! If you are inclined to take part in any activities that allow you to "make a killing", then grab the chance with both hands. Of course, you could channel that killer instinct into business ideas and make a killing that way.

How to Establish Your Purpose

First, decide. Simple, right? The key is to stop overthinking it and decide what drives you, inspires you, and ignites your passion. Do you have any talents that could be developed? Or you can take a different path. What do you fear, what makes your gut wrench and brings you out in cold sweats?

Take yourself out of the race for a while. Rent a cabin in the woods, dedicate an hour every morning to self-contemplation, or simply stroll through your neighborhood at night or whatever gives you the chance to think.

You won't have a clear plan initially; it will be muddied, blurry, and unclear. This should not stop you from acting on it. Elicit help from other alpha males, discuss your hopes and fears. True friends who already have a purpose will help you define your needs.

Do not waste time worrying about how your new purpose will impact your reality as that can be dealt with when the time is right. You are looking for something that will take you to higher levels of living.

Try These Simple Exercises to Help You Focus

1) *Write your own obituary*: Try not to think of this as a morbid exercise but as a way of "looking back" at what you have achieved. What is your legacy? What have you left behind as your personal footprint in history? People who work with terminally ill patients report that when the end is near, many of them are filled with regret at the end of their lives. They regret the times they spent worrying over trivialities and not focusing on things they wish they had done. Do not let that be you. How would you want to summarize the years you spent on Earth?

2) *Imagine a whole day free of responsibilities*: Being busy is a natural state for most people and can be worn as a badge of success. However, imagine a day when you don't have to go to work, there is no to-do list, and no one needs to see you. What is your instinct telling you to do? Maybe you feel you would benefit most from rest – a day spent chilling with Netflix may seem appealing. Now imagine you are fully rested before your free day, filled with energy and raring to go. Now, what do you imagine yourself doing? The choice is yours. Do you see yourself in the kitchen creating a new signature dish? Maybe you are out on the water perfecting your sailing skills. Money and time are no object. This is when you can let your imagination loose.

Make a Wish List

This is important. Making a physical note of a dream is an essential part of the transition from your mind to the real world. You now have something tangible to work with. Create an image on paper, put it in your eye line, and when life is throwing up challenges to test you, refer to your new inspiration. There is no timeline, just the knowledge that you will achieve whatever it is that gives you purpose.

Continue to forge ahead.

The first steps have been taken; now, your real journey begins.

Here are some of the pitfalls you will encounter along the way, and the different ways you will overcome them:

1) *You will step out of your comfort zone - way out.* Your comfort zone is a place that needs to be abandoned now and again. Only then will you experience the exhilaration of putting yourself out there.

2) *You will doubt yourself.* There will come a time when you need to make decisions that may take you to an uncertain conclusion. You can seek inspiration to lead you to the next step, or you can take a leap of faith. Even if you make a mistake, you will still learn from the experience.

3) *You will be tempted to bail.* When you strive for excellence, you will be tempted to reach a certain level and then stop. The purpose is a lifelong journey; there are no upper limits to your ambitions. The only reason to bail is if you feel you are on the wrong path, and you need to change direction.

4) *People will try and interfere.* Some people are destined to be ordinary, and that's okay. You have decided to be an alpha male, and not everyone will support you. You are soaring above them, and they will be looking to hold you back. Just keep your focus and ignore them; you are the master of your destiny.

5) *You will discover hidden resources.* You are standing on your own two feet, and that is empowering. Now is the time to dig down into your inner psyche and see what you can find. You are pushing yourself to higher planes; use your strength and courage to soar.

6) *You will meet like-minded people.* The road to discovery is filled with the coolest people. Here are creative types, visionaries, and people filled with purpose. You are in good company. Learn from them and embrace this brave new world.

7) *You will learn that your basic needs will be met.* No matter how much time and dedication you give to your new purpose, you will survive. You are an alpha male, and you know the importance of providing basic needs. You have an inbuilt ability to multitask, assigning time for essentials while making your dreams come true.

8) *You will wonder why you waited so long.* Once you are on the path to finding purpose, there will be a realization that the life you led before was unfulfilled. This should fill you with even stronger feelings

of hope for the future – just think about all the things you can achieve with your new attitude to life. This can apply to your professional life, social life, or hobbies. Whatever you choose to focus on, the choice is yours.

The main thing to learn from finding purpose is there are no limits to your success. Women love a man who believes in themselves; it means they will believe in them. You are that man; you refuse to be bound by traditional restraints.

Strategy 7: Chivalry

Chivalry has already been discussed as part of the discussion about what women want. However, modern men can often dismiss the art of chivalry as outdated and extinct. Studying the role of chivalry in history will help you recognize how it can be applied to modern romance.

The term originates in the 12th century by European knights. They covered issues about who should be spared and who it was okay to attack. These codes then filtered into society and became a law of war. It then faded but reappeared in the 18th and 19th centuries as a romantic vision of how men should treat women.

With the emergence of the First World War in 1914, the codes were once again militarized. They were depicted on wartime posters as knights riding into the battle with a noble cause. However, the real-life horrors of the conflict dispelled the notion of chivalry in war as returning soldiers told their tales of horror.

The idea that chivalry is dead is as old as the notion of chivalry. The alpha male knows that chivalry can be the perfect way to show a woman respect. He knows that his behavior towards her will determine what she does next. Trust your instincts and follow her lead. If she is determined to be a truly independent woman, you will soon get the hint.

The art of being a gentleman is not difficult and can prove to be one of your strongest assets.

Try these impressive chivalrous moves to wow her.

- *Food and drink*: Always offer her a drink or something to eat before you partake. This is good manners and should extend to everyone in your company.

- *Help her with her coat*: When it comes to removing her coat, you should offer assistance. Remove it and hang it in the appropriate place.

- *Seating*: Always stand behind her chair and pull it out for her to sit on. You should also do this for any other women who are unaccompanied. Never do it for accompanied women, though, if their guy is there – that's his job!

- *Ordering food*: When you are eating out, always wait for her to order her food before you order yours. If she asks you for advice, then you can share your preferences, but you should never offer suggestions without being asked.

- *Eye contact*: Make and maintain eye contact when speaking or listening to her. You should do this with all the people you are with; it displays an interest in their conversation.

- *Waiters*: If she expresses a need for a drink or maybe an item of cutlery, it is your job to catch the waiter's eye. Even if you are splitting the bill, it should be you who calls for it.

- *Coat*: When the time comes to leave, make sure you get her coat from the cloakroom and help her into it. Hold it open for her and let her slip her arms into the sleeves. You can then maneuver the shoulders into place and smooth the sleeves. This is an intimate gesture she will appreciate.

- *Keep her safe*: If you are entering a dark room or an unknown place, always take the lead. You are checking what perils lie ahead and keeping her behind your broad protective back. Normally you would allow her to enter a room first, but that only applies in a safe space.

- *Offer your arm*: When you extend your arm to a woman, you are assuming the role of protector. You are also showing her that you are part of her unit. A joint front is a strong front. Extend your arm when you are crossing uneven ground and give her an anchor to rely on.

- *Standing*: When a woman enters a room, standing up is a sign of respect. It doesn't matter if no one else respects this tradition. The fact that you do will register. As an alpha male, you are not afraid of bucking a trend. Stand up for her, smile, and say hello and you are guaranteed to pique her interest.

- *Tip your hat*: Okay, this is a little dated, but if you are wearing a hat, then tipping it is endearing as well as respectful. If you aren't wearing a hat, then tip your imaginary hat! Lift a finger to your forehead and give a jaunty tap. This is such a fun gesture that it will immediately get you noticed.

- *Cater to her needs*: At social events, it can be tricky to get noticed when you want a drink or snack. Always take the lead and make sure her every need is catered for. Stay by her side whenever possible, and make sure she is comfortable and enjoying herself. If you do have to speak to someone else, make sure she knows you are leaving. Don't just spot someone you need to see and leave her standing there.

- *Compliment her*: This is so important. You don't have to gush. Just notice something you genuinely admire about her. Maybe her hair looks amazing, or her scent is fabulous. Take the time to compliment her, and you will make her day.

- *Compliment her friends*: Women's friends are an extension of themselves, so when you compliment them, you compliment her. Now, no one is suggesting you make comments on their physical assets as that is a sure way of coming across as creepy. Instead, you should celebrate when something good happens to her friends. A new job, a change of boyfriend or a new apartment. Paying attention is the key. You are hardwired to be good to your partner, but being good to her friends is an extra step she will appreciate.

- *Keepsakes*: Women will often have mementos that remind them of special times. If you keep a memory alive by holding onto a theater ticket or even an old email, you are signaling you care about her. Just the tiniest indication you treasure the times you have spent together is worth a thousand words. This is a chivalrous habit that should never die!

Dancing

How many social interactions with women begin with a dance? Quite a lot, and knowing this means you should also be aware of social dance etiquette. You want to make an impression, but it needs to be the right one. You want to avoid looking like a jerk and enhance your reputation as a classy dancer. Imagine the scene: a group of women has spotted you across the room. A banging tune is being played, and they move en-masse to ask you to dance. Now learn the etiquette to make that scenario happen.

Tip 1: *Don't become a dance teacher.* Unless she hired you as a tutor, you should never critique your partner. Tell her she's a great dancer, she has amazing moves or simply let your feet do the talking. The purpose is to have fun, relax, and let the music wash over you both. Pointing out she has two left feet will not help you make your way back to her place.

Tip 2: *Never hit on a woman by asking them to teach you to dance.* You are not looking for a dance tutor; you are looking for a hookup! If you can't dance, take a class or study online. It is the man's responsibility to lead a dance move. They are expected to be confident and lead their partner.

Tip 3: *Don't squeeze her hand or anything else for that matter.* When you need to lead your partner away from a possible collision, you can increase the pressure on her hand. All other contacts should be light and caressing. You shouldn't be trying to impress her with your strength; the dance floor is all about grace. And it goes without saying that squeezing her butt is a surefire no-no.

Tip 4: *Don't be rough.* If you don't know what you're doing, the dancefloor can often turn into a borderline violent show of your strength. Some men think the only way to get their partners to follow them is to use force. Your skill should be enough to convey where she needs to be and when. You should be dancing with your partner, not wrestling with her! The trick is to use concentrated pressure to move your partner around the dancefloor.

Tip 5: *Don't out-dance your partner.* You may be the next John Travolta while she moves more like Dumbo on ice, but you shouldn't highlight the fact. If your partner is less skilled than you, then adjust your dance style to match hers. Check out how comfortable she feels by looking for facial clues. Frowning, crinkling of the eyes, and a look of terror are not good signs! The best leaders should be able to make any woman feel good no matter what their skill level.

Tip 6: *Don't dance when you are drunk.* In your head, you may feel like you are ready to take on the dancefloor in a huge dance-off competition. Alcohol has a way of lying to people about their dancing ability! If you know you have had a couple over your limit, then politely turn down any offers of dance until you feel soberer. You really don't want to be the guy crashing around, stepping on people's toes, and looking like a jerk!

Tip 7: *Don't make out on the dancefloor.* You know what can happen when you meet someone you like/lust after, and things get steamy. Dancing is an intimate experience, and things can often get heated. People get it; they just don't want to see it. If you want to get hot and heavy, then take it elsewhere. If you are in a bar surrounded by other couples grinding on each other, then suppose a certain amount of making out is okay, but you should still get a room. If you are at a family gathering or venue with serious dancers, this applies tenfold!

In conclusion: Etiquette is subjective. You need to know that not every woman will welcome it, and some will find it demeaning. Modern men are treading a thin line between chivalry and chauvinism. As an alpha male, it is important to recognize which is which.

As for the dancing, if it really is not your best feature, then consider classes or lessons. If the rhythm still fails to find you, then consider other ways to impress the ladies. Buy them a drink and wow them with your sparkling conversation instead.

Part 3: Seduction in Action

Choose Your Target

You are now primed for action, locked, and loaded. Your alpha male persona is ready to be unleashed on the female population. So what is next?

Understanding the types of women who are out there!

In today's world, every woman has her own unique qualities, and psychology specialists have narrowed down the categories to eight different types.

Type 1: The Playette

This type of woman is like a glorious iceberg. The parts you can see are stunning, but there is so much more under the surface. She doesn't wear her emotions on her sleeve and can often be difficult to spot. Other women will find her bitchy and hard to trust. She will have many male friends, some of whom she has dated in the past.

She always gets what she wants and is always looking for more. She wants to be swept off her feet initially and is looking for a man to rock her boat. She can be bored by traditional flirting, and she has seen it all before. You will need to surprise her, get her to let her guard down, and then swoop. Once she has allowed you in, you will find a sexy, exciting woman who is looking to connect on all levels. You need to get sexy fast without putting pressure on her.

What to look for when identifying a Playette: She will be modestly dressed, a great observer, in her early to mid-20s and generally in the company of men.

Type 2: The Social Butterfly

Also known as a party girl. She exists in her own bubble, and dating one takes a certain level of patience. They have a lot of friends but aren't super close to anyone. They will date for up to three months and then grow bored. Their social skills are fully developed while their other talents are less obvious. They love to be in the spotlight and will do almost anything to be noticed.

They are beautiful and charismatic, but they know it. They know they are enticing, and they will flirt outrageously. The difference between the Social Butterfly and the Playette is that the former loves to be the chaser. This can be off-putting to most men as they believe in traditional ways of dating. If you want to seduce a Social Butterfly, you need to show her your sexy, confident side. You need to let her chase you right up to the point when she falls into your bed! Don't expect anything long term; it may be brief, but it will be hot!

What to look for when identifying a Social Butterfly: She will be dressed to kill. Her hair, nails, and killer body will signal her confidence. She will be in a large social group and will flit from one person to the next. She can be any age but generally in her late 20s.

Type 3: The Hopeful Romantic

This type of personality is somewhat old fashioned. She is looking for a husband and a family. She will want a man who is sweet and romantic. This is not you! You are a highly developed alpha male who is not looking to settle. Move on and give this type a miss.

Type 4: The Cinderella

This type of woman is worth pursuing. She is beautiful but in a mature and evolved way. She will not be in the first flush of youth, but she has benefitted from her experiences. She will have had some disappointing and heart-breaking relationships in the past, but they will not stop her from dating. Her optimism is evident, and she still believes that men can be strong and sensitive. She is looking for great sex but hopes it will develop into a relationship.

The Cinderella type of woman will have very few female friends, but the ones she does have are loyal. She will have male friends but doesn't need to surround herself with them. She has her own methods of validating men; she is looking for confidence and strength.

What to look for when identifying a Cinderella: She will be more mature, so in her early thirties and onwards. She will be well groomed but understated. Her clothes will be classic and tailored while her makeup and hair will be immaculate. She will be in a small group or even just with another woman. You should begin by offering to buy her a drink as she has an old-fashioned perspective on dating.

Type 5: The Private Dancer

This type of woman has two distinct sides. In public, she is mysterious and alluring yet seemingly unapproachable. She gives out mixed signals, like a shy coy smile with a sexy glint in her eye. She is looking for a man to give her a wild ride in bed, but she will only show this side once she trusts you. Private Dancers are natural givers who enjoy a successful social life. They will have a close-knit circle of friends who have been together since college.

Once you get close to this type of woman, you will discover they have a whole other side to their personality. She is a horny woman who knows exactly what she wants. Mediocrity is not an option. You need to bring your A-game and bucketloads of energy. Strap yourself in for an experience you will not forget.

What to look for when identifying a Private Dancer: She will be in her mid to late thirties and will be successful in her chosen career. Her appearance will be classy and highly polished. She will be content to observe you from a distance while gauging your appeal. You will be aware of her scrutiny; use the opportunity to highlight your alpha male qualities. Show your sense of humor and your social confidence. Once the time is right, you should approach her and engage her in conversation. If she allows you to get close, she has already decided that you are worthy of her consideration.

Type 6: The Seductress

As the name suggests, this is a woman who is in the market for sex. The worst thing you can do when you pursue a Seductress is to believe she is easy. Forget that notion; this is one type of woman who knows what she wants and who should be giving it to her. This doesn't mean she doesn't have standards. She is looking for sex with no strings, not sex with just anyone. In fact, because of her confidence in her own appeal, a Seductress will have very high standards when it comes to choosing her next mate.

She will be drawn to your alpha male persona, but once you get past the physical attraction, you still need to keep her interested. This is when you can practice your rakish humor. Be as subtle or as obvious as you like. You won't shock her. She has heard every chat-up line, every sexual come on, and every compliment you can imagine. You will need to ignite her interest to get her into bed. You will not be disappointed; there will be no slow burn for her! Once you have registered on her radar, things will move quickly.

What to look for when identifying a Seductress: She will most likely be on her own. She doesn't need to hunt in a pack; the lone wolf effect appeals to her sense of urgency. If she meets a man that she wants to bed, she doesn't want to be hampered by her friends. She will be looking to connect, leave, and score! She will be dressed to show her best assets, maybe with a hint of sultriness. She will have elaborate makeup and perfectly coiffed hair. Her body language will ooze sexuality, and every touch will ignite your nerves. The Seductress can be any age, but the most successful ones will be in their thirties. At that age, they have the experience and confidence to know exactly who they are and what they want.

Type 7: The Connoisseur

This type of woman is not for the faint-hearted. She is looking for great sex with a strong sense of commitment afterward. One-night stands are not her style, and she is picky about her conquests. She loves to give. Once you have established a relationship with her, you are part of her personal circle, and she is generous to a fault. She will expect you to fight for her. After all, she is a prize worth winning. If you are looking for the ultimate challenge, then you should pursue this type of woman. Be warned, though, as she will expect commitment following sex. If you are willing to enter a relationship, then all will be well. If you expect to walk away after your first encounter, then you can expect not-so-pretty fireworks!

What to look for when identifying a Connoisseur: Age is not a factor with this type of woman. She could be heading for her forties or fresh out of college. She will be moderately dressed; she has no reason to send out signals. She will be part of a group that will be protective if you decide to approach her. The Connoisseur will have a sense of style in everything she does. Fine wines and dining experiences will interest her more than the bar scene.

Type 8: The Modern Woman

This is the type of woman who typifies the 21st century. She has a great job that allows her bags of independence both financially and timewise. She loves to date but is not looking for anything serious unless it just happens. She is more interested in your personality than your looks and is willing to mold a man to her expectations. The Modern Woman will also be willing to take the lead in the bedroom; she has a healthy respect for sex and knows her stuff. Looking for a man is not her first priority; she is more interested in fun. However, if the right man comes along, then she is all in!

What to look for when identifying a Modern Woman: She will probably be a member of a gym or dance class. Volunteering may also appeal to her; she has a healthy respect for people who are less well off than her. She is in her late twenties or early thirties and has a fresh, healthy look. The Modern Woman is confident in her looks without having to use obvious props. If you can't appreciate her natural beauty, then you are off her radar. She will appreciate a straight-talking man who looks her in the eye while chatting.

So, what is your type? You may be surprised at some of the types of women that are not on the list, but there is a reason for that. The bikini babe with the "banging rack" may not be a type, but you know they exist. As an alpha male, you may be expected to fall for this type of chick, but you know better. What you need is a challenge - not some bimbo who will be seduced by your physical attraction alone.

Also, there is a married woman. Off-limits, experienced, and up for horny times without any commitment. Yes, you can go there. Yes, it will set your heart racing, and your senses will be heightened - given all those secretive calls, and the hot and steamy hours spent wondering if you are going to get caught. The choice is yours, but if you do choose this path, take care. You may be a bad boy, but are you a homewrecker?

Fearless Flirting

Flirting with women is an art. It depends on the situation, the woman, and the preferred outcome.

Here are some strategies to help you make that important connection:

Project confidence. If you know what you are doing, you will put her at ease. Beautiful women get hit on a lot. There is a misconception that beautiful women are charmed by men who are so overcome with their beauty that they are left dumbstruck. This is not true. Men who blunder their way through a conversation are boring. Women want to be fascinated by you and find out more.

Initiate interesting conversations. When you talk to a woman, it can be easy to take over the conversation. You want her to be aware of your success, your interesting past, and your hopes and dreams for the future. But guess what? To her, that gets boring real fast if it is all that you are bringing to the conversation. Ask a woman about *her* and watch how she relaxes. As she lets down her barriers, she is allowing you insight into herself. This is an intimate gesture and means she's comfortable with you. Use your frame control to steer the conversation in the direction you want.

Use humor. When you flirt with a woman, you can come across as too intense. Yes, you are trying to get her into bed, but the best way to do so is to make her laugh. You shouldn't be crude or use toilet humor, but initiating amusing banter will make the conversation flow. Women love a man who can laugh with them; it creates all the right hormonal responses.

Gentle touching. A light touch on the arm can mean more than a hundred words. Wait for her to initiate personal touching and take her lead. This should be the most natural interchange in the world. If she starts to look creeped out, then back off at once.

Banter. You already know the power of humor, but banter takes it to a different level. You need to use the right phrases to avoid looking like an asshole. Try studying classic lines from the experts; use the films *It Happened One Night, Some Like It Hot,* and *Duck Soup* to perfect your badinage and comic timing. The key to great banter is to treat it like a tennis match. The comments should be back and forth and should be playful but not insulting. There is a risk you can get caught up in the moment and become overconfident. Or offending her and turning banter into a mockery. Make sure you have the art of banter mastered before you try it out.

The Art of Seduction by Text

When you have met a woman and sparked her interest, you need to maintain this even when you are apart. Text messages are a great way to make sure she remembers you, no matter how far away you are.

The blank text. How does sending a woman a blank text work? Well, you will pique her interest. She'll definitely send you one back asking if you made a mistake or if there is bad reception in your area.

If she finishes her text with a kiss and suggests you send one back, then try sending a blank text. When she comments on it, accuse her of being greedy by wanting two kisses back! Remember: Flirting is fun, so tease her and use humor to make her smile. If you do not have anything witty to say, just send a blank text. When she asks why you can just say that you gave her the silent treatment. Blank texts used to be accidental. Now they are one of the strongest teasing tools you have in your armory.

Next, how can you create sexual tension via text without flirting? Sexting!

Women love to know when you are thinking of them. If you know she is in a meeting or having a hard time at work, try to lighten the mood. Send her a cheeky emoticon that suggests you are imagining her romantically. Sexting is an art, and you need to know what is appropriate.

You can begin with cutesy kisses or even set the mood. Wine and music emoticons will tell her what she must look forward to. You can then take it up a notch – the lipstick and underwear emojis will tell her she should slip into something more comfortable, and sexy kisses and fireworks can indicate you are in the mood.

So, emoticons can be a really fun way to make a woman smile, but what if you prefer the written word?

Try These Sexy Texts to Get Your Woman in the Mood

There is nothing more beautiful than the thought of you wearing just the moonlight and my kisses.

I know you're having a busy week, but can I add one more thing to your to-do list? Me!

When you go to sleep tonight, imagine I am holding you tight.

You fill me with joy; I ache to see you again.

Words are powerful tools, and you can use them to crack even the hardest shell. Make her go all warm and fuzzy with just a couple of lines of text.

How to Flirt at the Grocery Store

Now you need to take a complete U-turn and perfect your flirting skills in a completely new environment. Bars, clubs, parties, and other social gatherings are meant to provide opportunities to meet women, but how many women go to the grocery store to meet guys? How many love stories begin with a tale of how their eyes met across a produce section? Not many. However, if you can perfect your skills there, then you are the alpha male who is always on the prowl.

Here is how you make the weekly grocery trip into another dating opportunity:

1) *Go to the same store at the same time every week.* The best time to go is just after work. The women who shop then will be less pressurized for time and more receptive to flirting. You may just establish eye contact the first week, followed by a cheeky nod the next. Week three, you can say something like, "We must stop meeting like this!" or something less cheesy!

2) *Try and break the ice.* Placing bananas in the child's seat of your trolley is the perfect way to attract attention. Once you see they are looking, you can open a conversation. "It's okay. I haven't got kids. I'm thinking of adopting these cheeky yellow guys" or "I've put them there to stop them from getting squashed. Do you think they'll be okay?" Ice breaker completed! Humorous conversation established.

3) *Spot the single ladies.* Women who shop together often live together or are single. Roomies will shop in pairs to avoid doubling up on common items. Single women will often shop with friends, while women with boyfriends tend to shop alone or with their partner.

4) *Check out the fruit and vegetable aisle.* The world is living in an era of healthy eating and embracing whole foods. If you are perusing the fresh produce section, you are sending out a message, *Look, ladies, I care about my body and only feed it wholesome stuff!* The produce aisle also offers a place to initiate innocent physical contact. If you are both reaching for a juicy mango and your fingertips just happen to brush against hers, then make eye contact, smile, and start a conversation!

5) *The checkout line is your new best friend.* Think about it. Everyone is standing in a line waiting to pay for their stuff. You have a rack of tabloid magazines to look at. Try initiating a conversation about a cover. Maybe she has something in her basket that is a bit unusual, papaya or artichoke will do. Ask her how she cooks with it, as you have been meaning to try it but aren't sure what to do with it. This is a great way to suggest a date. Does she fancy a coffee while you swap recipes? Again, the ice has been broken, and conversation will follow.

Flirting is not just about attracting women; it is about making the other person feel better about themselves. Use flirting techniques to interact with other people you meet, and your techniques will go from strength to strength. When you become a master at flirting, you will also become the guy everyone wants to speak to. You make people feel good, and everyone can benefit from a little feel-good time.

Dating Linguistics

Human language is complex. It is used to convey a variety of emotions, desires, and hypotheses to others. There are different branches of linguistics, but this book concentrates on dating and how to express your desires in a subtle, understated way while making your intentions crystal clear. You want this woman, now learn how to let her know!

NLP Seduction Techniques

Neuro-Linguistic Programming (NLP) is a relatively new area of science that studies social approaches and their successes. It focuses on a set behavior and how this affects the person being targeted.

The best way to explain is to give examples.

Example 1: Mirroring. This is a technique that has been touted for years by dating gurus. They tell you to be like the girl by copying her actions, and she will form a rapport with you. Well, to an extent, this is correct, but with one major twist.

If you copy a girl's actions immediately after they have performed them, they will soon catch on. Instead of feeling rapport, they will see you as a needy, desperate guy.

Instead, you need to mirror the action after a slight delay. So, imagine you are talking to a girl in a bar, and she scratches her nose. You then wait three seconds and scratch your own nose. She may have altered her stance by then; maybe she has leaned on the bar. You wait three seconds, and then you lean on the bar.

Mirroring is all about rapport, the tone of voice, her breathing pattern, and even her eye movements. Once you are in simpatico, she will begin to see the similarities between the two of you and then... Boom!

Example 2: Create a memory. Now is the time to get inventive. As you feel your conversation coming to an end, you need to make sure she remembers you. Link the time you have spent together with an object and give her a tangible reminder to keep.

For instance,

You say, "I had such fun chatting with you; I hope we can do this again."

She says, "Me too; I'm sure we will run into each other again."

Now, at this point, you run the risk of being forgotten once she leaves the room. Try this technique to make a memory.

You say, "Well, I sure hope so. Tell you what, let's take all that fun we had and put it in this napkin." Then you put the imaginary fun into the napkin and fold it. "Whenever you need it, you can pick this up, open it and remember the fun we had." You could also use the opportunity to write your number or email on the napkin.

Now, this may seem a bit cutesy and new worldly, but it works. Instant nostalgia mixed with a productive connection will mean she is thinking of you all day.

Example 3: Turn negativity into a positive emotion. When you are talking to a woman, it can be awkward when the subject of an ex or a bad break up arises. Some men are overwhelmed when strong emotions are expressed and will back off.

Try this technique instead.

She is telling you how much of a jerk her last boyfriend was. He cheated on her, lied to her, and she is getting angrier. She is in an emotional state that is not conducive to flirting, so how do you change that?

Try this.

"Wow, he sounds like a real dirtbag. He didn't deserve a beautiful woman like you. He certainly doesn't deserve the chance ever to hurt you again. Here, take this piece of paper (you then hand her a sheet of paper) and pretend this is him. Crumple up that jerk and make him feel small. Put all your anger into that paper, rip it to shreds, and then toss it into the trash. You never have to deal with that guy again."

Chances are she will now be going at it with enjoyment. Ripping that paper and dumping it will help her move from a negative state of mind into a more positive state. And guess who she will associate with the termination of these negative thoughts? You! She will love you for it!

So, how do you also turn a negative situation into a positive sexual encounter?

As an alpha male, you are pursuing only the top level of women, the chicks all the other men lust over, but you will come across a common response: The "I have a boyfriend" scenario. Attractive women will often claim to be attached just to see how interested you are. Are you willing to continue your pursuit, or will you fall at the first hurdle?

You are alpha; first hurdles are a breeze for you. Try this technique to create a lasting impression.

You have just been told by the hot lady you have your eye on that she is attached. Do you walk away? No, try the following response:

"That's great. Isn't it amazing when you have that sort of connection? I love being in a relationship, that passionate feeling you find at the base of your stomach when you are in their company. The hot trail it leaves through your body as it makes its way to the top of your head is awesome. Do you mind if I ask you how you feel when you are with your boyfriend?"

Hopefully, she will say:

"Well, I feel a fluttering sensation in my stomach that travels both up and down my body. My senses are alight, and my breathing becomes hot and heavy."

Now you have helped her relive how she feels when aroused. You can follow it up with:

"Wow, that's interesting. You feel it right there (then lightly touch her stomach), and then it travels to your throat (lightly touch her throat)."

You have now relived the feeling of attraction with your nonverbal cue. Job done. Where this goes from here is up to the two of you. She may or may not be attached; that does not matter. She certainly knows who you are and what you are capable of!

Flirting in the Modern World

You will be aware of the old-fashioned cheesy pickup lines used by lesser males: "Do you come here often?" or "Are you tired? You've been running through my mind all night." And yes, some women might find them endearing, but the majority will just give you a withering look and leave.

Flirting is not about using lines; it is about making them feel good about themselves while initiating contact. In the modern world, it can be as simple as exchanging social media details. Ask her if she is on Facebook or Instagram and ask for her details. If she does not feel comfortable doing that, then give her yours.

Asking for someone's phone number is also another way to get her attention. Try asking for her digits instead and make yourself stand out from the crowd. If you have a card or piece of paper with your number on it, you can give her the option to call you. Women sometimes prefer having this option.

Use the phrase "I love your..."

This is not as creepy as you think. Begin with something innocent and cute like their eyes, dress, or laugh. If you prefix your comment with the phrase "Can I just say", you are making it less aggressive.

For instance,

You say: "Can I just say I love your eyes."

She says: "Thank you."

You reply: "They are so bright; they light up your face."

This is a softer approach than going in with a hard approach.

If you are more comfortable flirting using compliments, another great phrase to use is "Has anyone ever told you".

It not only allows you to insert a flattering compliment, but it also keeps the conversation flowing. Asking a question is much more likely to command a response.

When you are talking to a woman, and she indicates she is not seeing anyone, you can turn that into a compliment as well. "How are you still single?" will make her feel better about being unattached and also get a response.

Dating Linguistics is all about making the lady in question feel good about herself. Use affirmative language and compliments without seeming too obvious. You are an attractive alpha male who knows how to flirt like a professional. What can go wrong?

Learn to accept rejection: A real man knows how to accept defeat and move on with grace. Hopefully, the ladies will be gentle when turning you down, allowing you to thank them for their time and leave. Even if they are downright rude, you should still be gracious. Keep your tone light and your responses measured. Even bad boys know how much good manners matter.

Sack Hacks: Tips to Get Her to Sleep with You Instantly

Now you come to the bottom line: Sealing the deal. Whatever way you put it, the whole point of seduction is getting the chick to sleep with you. You may view this as a one-off experience, or it may be the beginning of a beautiful relationship. The first time you sleep with a woman can dictate what happens afterward, so it is important to get it right!

Make Your Bedroom a Sexier Place

If you are trying to convince a woman to get naked and do the horizontal tango with you, they may be put off by a boudoir that is distinctly unsexy! Setting the scene will at least give you a fighting chance of success.

Remove objects that focus on yourself: The idea is to create a couple's paradise, but if your personal objects surround you, the mood can soon dip. If the walls of your bedroom are littered with diplomas and certificates, then take them down. Any exercise equipment should also be removed. You don't want her focusing on these "selfish objects" when her focus should be on you.

Keep your technology out of sight: Have you ever been interrupted mid-move by a beeping phone? Not sexy, right? Both of you should be free from devices when you enter the bedroom.

Remove dirty washing: This is a two-part exercise. You need to get rid of actual dirty washing. There is nothing more off-putting than smelly socks and underwear on the bedroom floor. Take any hampers and put them in the bathroom. Secondly, remove any pictures of former girlfriends – you don't need to air your dirty washing in front of a new conquest.

Create a sexy smell: It is a proven fact that women respond to smells. Aphrodisiac oils like jasmine and sandalwood can lift the room. A couple of drops on a pillow will help your date relax.

Now you need to get the girl back to your bedroom. How do you do that? Well, you will use all the things covered so far.

Imagine the scene:

You have locked eyes with the cute blonde in the tight dress, which is the center of attention among her friends. You decide there is a definite attraction between the two of you, so you head over. You have defined her as a party girl; her age, demeanor, and actions tell you that this is a woman who may be up for some fun.

As you reach her side, you smile and tilt your head. You observe her reactions. She flutters her eyelashes and takes a drink without breaking eye contact. All good so far. Your body language is open and confident as you lean in and say, "Hi."

The two of you are acting as if the rest of the room does not exist. There is a sizzling tension between you, so what happens next? You need to build on this initial tension and up the stakes. Take your finger and brush it across the back of her hand. This simple gesture has no sexual overtones in the real world, but you two are far beyond this reality. That simple gesture will have her panting for more. After your initial touch, you need to see if she responds with a caress. If she is interested, she will find some way to initiate a situation that requires physical contact.

Now the flirting is reaching a crescendo. You are both using banter to tease each other and create sexual innuendoes. You are at your most manly. She is a woman who is responding to her basic urges, so the outcome should be natural. You take her hand, lead her to the door, and the rest is just natural.

How to Make Emotional Connections

Your key skill when persuading women to sleep with you is to make an emotional connection. You can get them interested in your physical beauty, your humor, and expert flirting. And yes, for some women, that will be enough. However, the best sex comes with an emotional attachment. When you both feel connected, the sex can be mind-blowing.

Women will test you endlessly. Beautiful women have heard all the cheesy lines before. They know how gorgeous they are, they know they have great bodies, so why not try another tactic. Imagine beautiful women with balloons attached to their arms. When other men come to them and compliment them about how amazing they are, the balloon inflates.

Imagine what would happen if you busted her chops and teased her. When you pop that balloon, you get her attention. If she is so humorless that she cannot cope with a bit of teasing, then she is not worth your time anyway. A woman with a sense of humor will recognize your tactic and enjoy the verbal banter.

Getting women to sleep with you should not be that difficult. They are sexual creatures, so they too are seeking satisfying sexual encounters, so why aren't you getting laid?

1) *You are boring.* You work, you provide, and you look for sex/relationships. So, what do you talk to chicks about? If all you can talk about is what happened at work today, then she is bound to lose interest. Keep up with the news and read online articles about interesting developments in the world. Watch top rated television shows and movies, as media is a popular subject to chat about. There are no concrete rules about what you should talk about, but you

should be passionate about subjects. If you are animated about your passions, you will become more interesting to her.

2) *You are trying too hard*: You are a man's man. You like to watch sports, drink beer, and hang out with like-minded dudes. That's fine; women happen to like masculine men. If you then decide to take up watercolor painting or Pilates to impress the ladies, you will come across as fake. Yes, you should widen your horizons, yes you should take up hobbies that make meeting women easier but only choose stuff that is genuinely interesting to you.

3) *You are in the friend zone*: You need to know the difference between a good friend and a potential love interest. If you are overly friendly and treat her like a princess, then you are unlikely to make her hot and horny, and thus, she won't take her clothes off. You need to signal your interest straight away. Actively trigger the sexual tension already discussed; be masculine, charming, and sexually confident. If you already know the woman in question, as a friend, yet you want to upgrade the relationship, then you should be clear and honest with her about it. Tell her that you feel a more intimate relationship could be on the cards. If you do it correctly, then you should be able to maintain the friendship even if she rejects you.

4) *You give up too early*: Women want a man who is confident, safe, and capable of protecting them. They will often play hard to get in order to test that confidence. They will run hot and cold. They will ignore you and talk to other men. These are tests to gauge how interested you are. Just smile, relax, and show her you are still there. Beautiful women know how desirable they are and will only let the prime examples of manhood get near them.

5) *You rely on your looks*: Okay, you have worked on perfecting your alpha male body, and this will help you get noticed. Less attractive or downright ugly women will find this enough and still sleep with you, but hot women need more! You need to charm her, be witty, and be genuinely interested. Never rely on a fake persona; be yourself, and if she doesn't respond, then move on.

6) *You believe women give out signs*: It can be difficult to know when it's okay to make a move. You can spend too much time looking for obvious signs that she is interested. All women are different; some will be only too happy to signal their availableness while others will wait for you to make the first move. Make that leap of faith, ask for her number, or if you can buy her a drink. What's the worst that can happen?

The trouble with rejection is that it can affect even the most confident man. So, stop the rejection now! You need to boost that self-confidence with a win. Put on that winning smile, dress that hot bod in your best threads, and get out there. There are masses of hot women just waiting to jump your bones, so do not disappoint them! Get busy!

The Chase

Face it: Dating is heavily weighted on the side of the woman. She makes all the choices. After all, she has men falling at her feet just waiting to date her, right? Well, what if you could turn the tables? Once you have established that she is interested, how do you turn this interest into desire? How do you make her crave the very touch of you until she cannot think of anything else?

Follow these simple do's and don'ts to make her want you more than chocolate!

1) *Ask the right questions:* Do not be a douche. She will assume you are one, and you don't want to prove her right. Never ask stupid questions. Cheesy pick-up lines are okay further down the line when you are ironically cute. Lines like "Hey babe, what does it feel like to meet the man of your dreams?" will make her reach for the sick bag. Ask her what her dreams and ambitions are and let her talk. Women are not interested in hearing how great you are – leave them to work that out by themselves!

2) *Don't linger:* You had a life before you met her, so carry on with it. Meet with your friends and go to the game. If you drop all your plans every time she calls, you will soon become boring. Women want a challenge. Give her a reason to up her game. If she wants to distract you from important sports, then she will need to make it very clear

what you would be missing! Avoid long conversations on the phone. Say what you want and then hang up. Never do the "You put the phone down first" thing. That's for teenagers and soppy guys. If you are brief without being rude, she will soon wonder why. If you do text her late at night, just do it once or twice. Make it clear you have other things in your life, and she will soon be chasing you for your time.

3) *Challenge her.* Most women expect you to regard them as the best thing that's ever happened to you. Try something different and watch her reaction. Have a light jokey conversation about dating and ask her why she thinks she's better than the girls you have dated previously. She will be taken aback at first but will relish the opportunity to back herself. You can take the conversation one step further by pointing out your own qualities compared to the guys she has dated. This may seem harsh, but you are only trying to have an honest conversation with her. Keep her on her toes and remind her what a catch you are!

4) *Listen and remember.* Most men let women ramble on about their work, friends, and family while only half-listening. So what happens if you become the ultimate listener? You take the time and energy to remember what she told you. Use these snippets of information to initiate conversations. Try asking questions based on what she told you. For instance, "Hey, how did that project you were working on with Sally work out? Did you get it finished in time?" or "Hey, how did your mother cope with her dental appointment? Did she have to get any further work done?" You will soon become the person she wants to share her conversations with because you are such a good listener.

5) *Surprise her.* When you are listening to her, pick up on certain facts, and then use them to surprise her. For instance, she may mention how much she loved a certain candy bar when she was younger. Leave it a couple of weeks and then show up with that certain candy bar as a gift. Gestures like these will drive her wild. They are more intimate and special than any roses or jewelry. You are the guy who remembers tiny details, and she will not want to lose that guy.

6) *Master your look*: The eyes are the window to the soul, and if you can get them to speak, the ladies will come running! Practice a look that screams, "I want you. Now. Right here." Learn from the masters; Johnny Depp and Ryan Gosling can both make women melt with just a stare.

On the other side of the coin, a boring look can be just as effective. If you feel a woman is losing interest in your conversation, then let your eyes wander. Ask her to repeat what she said as you were distracted. Now, if she is bored with you, this will wrap up the conversation quickly. If she were testing you, it would give her a shock as she needs to start paying more attention, or she may lose you!

7) *Be the positive force in her life*: If you whine about work or your friends, you will seem like just any other guy. If, however, you are always upbeat, a shining beacon of positivity that is always ready to see the silver lining, she will seek you out. Who does she know who always makes her feel better about herself? You, that's who. Women love to have a positive man to lean on when they hit the roadblocks that life loves to lay down!

8) *Hold your ground*: Don't be a lap dog. Have your own opinions, and never bow down to hers just to get on her good side. She will appreciate your intelligence and honesty. The debate can be sexy; heated conversations can lead to other heated activities. By showing her that you have your own opinions, you are telling her she can rely on you for an honest opinion. This will make her turn to you when she has an important decision to make.

9) *Create mystery*: Suggest that she reminds you of the female lead in your favorite romance novel. Think about it. You are paying her a compliment; most women would love to be the lead character in a romantic novel. Next, you are showing your softer side by revealing you like to read romantic novels. She will, of course, want details, so do your research. Pick a novel that has been made into a feature film and start taking notes! Be cagy about the details and tease her into wanting more!

10) *Make everything you do enjoyable*: Make your dates exciting; everyone can do dinner and a movie, but what can you do to make her head spin? Try these different date ideas to keep her interested.

- **Look for treasure.** Browse yard sales, markets, antique shops, and secondhand stores. You can marvel over the best bargains and make the date fun and frugal!
- **Rent a boat for the afternoon.** There is something about a boat that yells romance. You may feel a sailboat is beyond your skill set, but don't let that put you off. Try a kayak or paddleboat; the idea is to spend time on the water floating lazily together.
- **Do some stargazing.** Buy a book on constellations, grab a picnic and blanket, and camp out on a hill. Imagine the scene... a warm summer night, a chilled bottle of wine with two glasses, nibbles, and the night sky. What woman can resist that?! If the weather isn't the best, then take a more professional approach and visit the planetarium.
- **Take her to a festival.** Depending on your comfort level, you can choose to camp or book an expensive hotel nearby. The music is what matters. Shared experiences are a sign you are investing in the relationship, and this will keep her coming back for more.
- **Bowling.** This is a classic date night that is seeing a resurgence. Fun, competitive, and sporty – this is a great idea for a first date. If you win, you get to give her a consolation hug, and if you lose, you get to give her a victory hug. Bowling may not seem to be the ideal venue for physical contact, but you know different!

The main point to take away from these tips is to stop doing the chasing. Women like to be pursued – of course they do! They expect it, so imagine the intrigue when you refuse to play along.

Other men have an air of desperation when they approach women. You, on the other hand, have an air of entitlement. You are an alpha male who should be recognized as a prime specimen. You are expecting these women to find you attractive and act accordingly, and you will find that they will.

Be the best version of yourself and get ready to have hordes of females beating a path to your door!

Iron Rules All Men Should Follow

Why should you follow the rules? You are the alpha male; surely, it is your job to make the rules? Well, actually, rules are the backbone of every successful operation, and seduction/dating is no different. All sportsmen know the value of guidelines and rules. Male politicians and businessmen abide by strict protocols that are meant to keep them focused, so why not apply the same principles to all men?

Here are the Iron Rules for Success

#1 *Believe in yourself:* If you are doubtful, then you project unease. Confidence is part of your wardrobe, so wear it well. Your self-belief should be evident without it seeming like cockiness. Everything you do should indicate your alpha status.

#2 *Project your frame:* This strategy was covered earlier, but it is worth repeating. When you control the frame, you are prepared for everything. Losing track of a conversation or situation can make you look weak. The only time you want to look weak is when you decide to let a woman see your vulnerable side. You have the verbal skills to direct conversations; you also know when to keep quiet and listen. Your frame is important; use it well and be the master of all interactions.

#3 *If a woman is making you wait for sex, then walk away.* She is trying to make you feel inferior. Trying to take the upper hand is okay when she is dealing with beta or omega males, but alpha males are superior. If she is indicating her lack of interest in sealing the deal, then the sex is probably not worth it. She will be the one who is missing out, so move on and pick a woman who is worthy of your attention.

Women who are confident in bed rarely make men wait. This doesn't mean they are easy – quite the opposite. They only choose men who can match their expectations, but once they have, the action will heat up very quickly. They know what to expect and see no point in waiting.

#4 *Men and women shouldn't live together unless they are married.* Your home is your castle, and unless you have found your queen, why would you share it? Male housemates are okay; they can be buddies who are fun to hang with. Women don't want to hang; they want to talk about feelings and share their lives with you.

If you are dating, you need somewhere to escape to. A male-orientated den that is fueled by testosterone will help you regain your alpha status after a touchy-feely date! If you are planning to marry a woman, then you should live together for a few months just to make sure you are compatible.

Other than that, there are no circumstances whatsoever when you should live with a woman. If the woman you are dating finds herself in need of new accommodation due to unforeseen circumstances, then fine. Help her find a new place ASAP or remind her that her friends are in a better position to help.

#5 *Never get trapped by women.* Always take control of birth control. Yes, it can be restricting to wear protection, but it is necessary. Women will tell you they have it covered, and maybe they do – or maybe they are looking for a chance to get their claws into you. There are options, but condoms are the go-to method of preventing pregnancy. They also protect you from sexually transmitted diseases like herpes and chlamydia.

Make sure your condoms are getting the job done by following these simple rules.

• Always use latex or polyurethane condoms that have been stored in a cool dark place. Other forms of condoms may not give you the same level of protection against diseases.

• Check the expiration date. Making sure your condom is in date will stop any breakages or spills.

• Use water or silicone-based lubes. Oil-based lubes can affect the condom and cause problems.

• Never carry your condoms in your wallet. The friction and heat can damage them.

#6 *Take care of your body.* This is an obvious one, and the exercises covered will help you keep physically fit. However, some alphas don't realize the importance of overall health. Watch your diet and hydrate regularly. Be aware of nutrition levels and how foods affect your body. You also need to be aware of your mental health. You can't have a healthy mind in an unhealthy body.

Listen to what your body is telling you. Make sure you have regular checkups with your doctor and dentist. There is no point in having a kick-ass body with dreadful teeth. Your smile is the focal point of your face; look after it! Also, your mouth is the source of a serious amount of pleasure, so take care of it!

Never underestimate colds or fatigue; they can both be a sign that something else is wrong. Think of your body as a machine. Keep maintenance levels high and be mindful of what fuel you supply it with!

#7 *Always look forward.* Alphas always have goals. They reach them, complete them, and then move forward. Perspective is key. You need targets, or you can find yourself waltzing through life without achieving anything. Karma will not decide your fate; you will.

The same rule applies to relationships. If you find your current relationship reaching a natural conclusion, then end it. The best way to do this is to be honest and final. Tell her how much you've loved your time together, but it is time to move on. Resist any temptation to give it another go. You know when it is time to move on, so don't be sentimental and stay when you know that the end is inevitable.

#8 *Never go back*: Once you have moved on, keep it that way. You can stay friends with your ex but never go back for sex. You are just scratching an itch, but she will feel false hope. An alpha man will never need sex so much they use someone they once dated to satisfy a need. Move on; there are women out there just waiting to hook up with you.

#9 *Never quantify*: No matter the pressure, never reveal the number of women you have slept with in the past. This applies to both male and female friends. That information is yours and is not for sharing. You should also keep details of particular sexual experiences private.

Men talk about sex. Women talk about sex. It is only natural, and it's also healthy. What is not healthy is telling tales out of school. When you sleep with a woman, it's a personal, intimate experience. It doesn't matter if you are together for one hour, one night, or for years – you don't share your experiences with anyone. When you talk about sex, keep it vague, and never name names.

#10 *You will never understand women completely*: It is a fact. Women are another species and have totally different ways of thinking. This is okay; it's all part of the adventure. As an alpha, you will know more about women than most men, and that is what makes you stand out from the crowd.

Understand that women are the primary sexual selectors and let them keep that position. You give them all the information they need. You are a prime specimen and should be on their radar, but accept that sometimes you may not be the man she wants.

Women will never be able to love their men in a way that they expect. The sooner you accept that fact, the better. You have an idealized idea of true love, and women have another. The best you can hope for is a successful mix of the two strategies. Never become disillusioned with women; they can't help how they are put together!

#11 *Never self-deprecate:* Dating sites will often tell you to show your soft side, admit your failings, and appeal to her sympathies. This is a crock! Sympathy should only be found in a dictionary between shame and syphilis. If you think looking pathetic is attractive, then be prepared to spend a serious amount of time "self-loving" your family jewels!

Women may throw you a pity sex session, but you will always be the sad sack who is needy. There's nothing worse for an alpha male than taking the route of self-deprecation.

#12 *Quality over quantity:* This is an important rule as it applies to all aspects of life. Food should be of high quality and nutritional. Clothing should be classic and high quality. Your actions and activities should be tempered to meet this rule. If you are asked to attend numerous functions, only choose the ones that benefit your social life.

And, of course, women! Do you really want to sleep with different women every night by lowering your standards? Or would you rather have classy women once a month? The choice is yours, but the answer should be obvious!

The bottom line is that you may play by these rules, but you also make them. You are the man, the alpha, and you will not be dictated to by anyone!

Conclusion

You are now on your way to become a complete alpha male. Women are waiting for you. Other men will be in awe of you. You know the important things there is to know about women.

Remember that dating and seduction should be fun! Yes, women is a serious business when you are not getting any, but you now have the skills to make sure you are.

You are the leader, so get out there and do your thing!

Check out another book by Kory Heaton

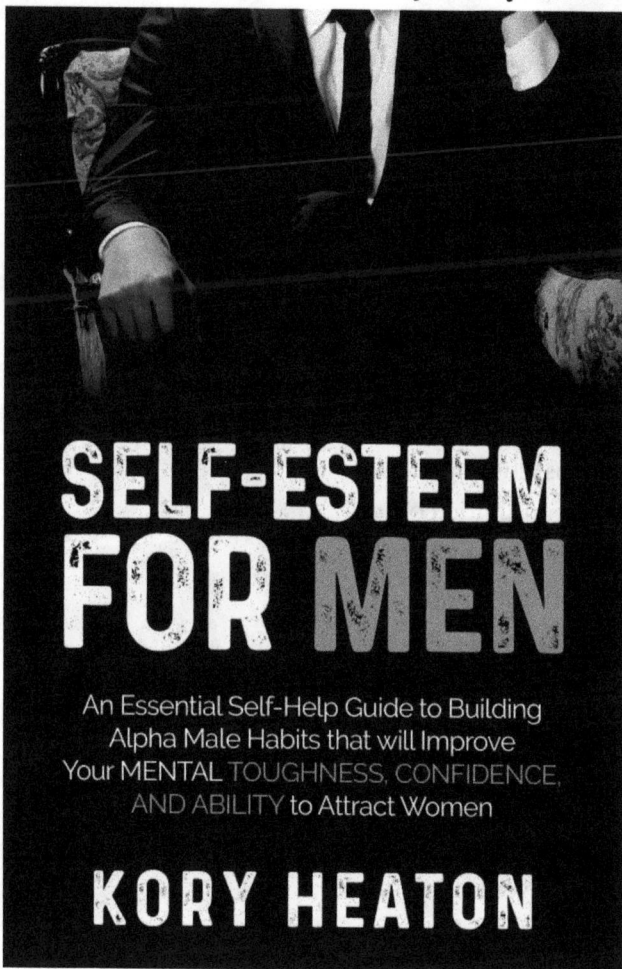

SELF-ESTEEM FOR MEN

An Essential Self-Help Guide to Building Alpha Male Habits that will Improve Your MENTAL TOUGHNESS, CONFIDENCE, AND ABILITY to Attract Women

KORY HEATON

Acknowledgments

http://www.braveworld.com

http://www.stanfordedu.com

http://www.elitedaily.com

http://www.smh.com

http://www.waytoosocial.com

http://www.theclever.com

http://www.psychologytoday

http://www.tomsguide.com

http://www.lovepanky.com

http://www.sosuave.com

http://www.monday.com

http://www.uncagedman.com

http://www.evolvedwoman.com

http://www.selfgrowth.com

http://www.seductionscience.com

http://www.modernman.com

http://www.prevention.com

http://www.charlesedge.com

http://www.luvze.com

http://www.alphamale.com

http://www.heartofcharm.com

http://www.brobible.com

http://www.enlightenmentportal.com

http://www.mantelligence.com

http://www.redpilltheory.com

http://www.girlchase.com
http://www.brainadd.com
http://www.guysplaybook.com
http://www.derekrake.com
http://webiferview.com
http://www.adaringadventure.com
http://www.winwithwomen.com
http://www.emlove.com
http://www.medium.com